STRIP-PIECED QUILTS

Easy Designs from Just Six Fabrics

MAAIKE BAKKER

Martingale®
& COMPANY

That Patchwork Place® is an
imprint of Martingale & Company®.

Martingale & Company
20205 144th Avenue NE
Woodinville, WA 98072-8478 USA
www.martingale-pub.com

Printed in China
10 09 08 07   8 7 6 5 4

Library of Congress Cataloging-in-Publication Data
Bakker, Maaike.
    Strip-pieced quilts / Maaike Bakker.
        p. cm.
    ISBN 978-1-56477-639-6
    1. Patchwork—Patterns. 2. Patchwork quilts.
3. Strip quilting. I. Title.
    TT835.B2635 2005
    746.46'041—dc22
                                        2005016002

Mission Statement

Dedicated to providing quality products
and service to inspire creativity.

Credits

President ❖ Nancy J. Martin
CEO ❖ Daniel J. Martin
VP and General Manager ❖ Tom Wierzbicki
Publisher ❖ Jane Hamada
Editorial Director ❖ Mary V. Green
Managing Editor ❖ Tina Cook
Technical Editor ❖ Ellen Pahl
Copy Editor ❖ Sheila Chapman Ryan
Design Director ❖ Stan Green
Illustrator ❖ Robin Strobel
Cover Designer ❖ Shelly Garrison
Text Designer ❖ Regina Girard
Photographer ❖ Brent Kane

ACKNOWLEDGMENTS

You never write a quilt book on your own. There are many others behind the scenes who assist in numerous ways. Thanks to:

Joke Griffioen, Anja Jalving, Ineke Jongens, Aletta Kwant, Frouk van der Molen, Bartina Noorman, Els Oosterloo, Marijke Schortinghuis, Elly Weteling, and Tineke Zweers for their help in making the quilts and for their warm support

Wim Dooren, for taking my photograph

Theo Claas, my husband, for doing the word processing and the first editing

My children, for their patience

Contents

Introduction

Strip piecing is an excellent technique for making quilt tops in a fast and easy way. You don't need to make templates—just cut strips using rotary-cutting tools, sew the strips together, and cut the strip sets again into squares or other shapes.

All the beautiful and exciting quilts in this book are based on the same four basic steps:

* First, choose six fabrics in color gradations or in colors that are next to each other on the color wheel.

* Second, cut these fabrics into strips of equal width.

* Third, sew the strips together into strip sets, either in two groups of three or with all six strips together, in order from the lightest to the darkest fabric.

* Fourth, cut the strip sets into squares, 60° triangles, quarter-square triangles, or oblique squares to create blocks. Then simply play with the blocks until you have arranged a quilt top that pleases you. Sew the blocks together.

This book is suitable for beginning quilters as well as for more experienced quilters. Beginners will love how easy strip piecing is to learn, and they'll appreciate the clear, simple instructions for cutting, sewing, and quilting. But this book can also be appealing and challenging for more advanced quilters because of the opportunities to experiment and learn about color, value, and design. You can use the blocks you create to make quilts similar to those shown in this book, or use them to make your own unique and original quilt designs.

I have shared my enthusiasm about strip piecing with many students, and they love the technique and the quilt designs. It was their enthusiasm that inspired me to write this book. I hope that you, too, will become enthusiastic about strip piecing and my quilt designs. Give it a try and you'll be astonished and surprised at the many creative possibilities.

Maaike Bakker

Choosing Fabric

When you select colors and fabrics, the most important thing is to have courage. Select fabrics in colors that you like, keeping in mind the decor surroundings and the function of the quilt. However, don't try to make the colors match perfectly; your quilt may end up dull and monotonous. Be sure you have good contrast where needed. Don't hesitate too long—your first color choice is often the best one. A quilt often becomes a great quilt when it includes an unexpected color.

COLOR AND TONAL VALUE

All the quilts in this book are made of six different fabrics, either in gradations of a color (one color that goes from light to dark) or in colors that create a rainbow or part of a rainbow. Those would be colors that flow from one to the other on the color wheel.

Some knowledge about tonal value is also important. Tonal value is the degree of darkness or lightness in color. White is the lightest tonal value and black is the darkest. All other colors fit somewhere between these two. You can create a tonal scale by arranging colors according to lightness and darkness. Printed fabric can also be arranged in a tonal scale.

Gradations of one color

Part of a rainbow

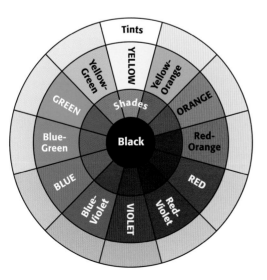

Printed fabrics arranged in tonal value from light to dark

You can check the tonal scale by arranging the fabrics from light to dark; then look at the fabrics by squinting or looking through a camera. This will give you a distance perspective and let you see value differences. For best results, be sure there is sufficient contrast between the fabrics. You don't want the fabrics to be too similar in tonal value. There should be contrast either between light and dark colors or between complementary colors. You can check the contrast also by squinting or looking through a camera. Good contrasts will remain visible if you look with one of these methods.

When you don't want to have sharp definition between the strips, try fabrics with large-scale prints. The colors will flow from one to another.

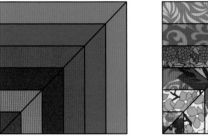 

BORDER FABRIC

The border of a quilt is like the frame around a painting. It separates the quilt from its surroundings and should make the center of the quilt shine. I like to use relatively dark colors for the borders. A darker border lets your quilt sparkle. I often select the darkest color used in the quilt as a starting point when selecting the fabric for the border.

I often add a narrow, brightly colored strip as an inner border to connect the elements in the center of the quilt. It ties the colors together, like a rope wound around the blocks of the quilt. In addition, it can place emphasis on certain colors used in the quilt, and it

can also add that unexpected element that makes your quilt an exciting one.

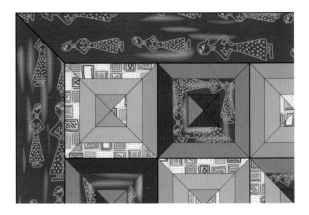

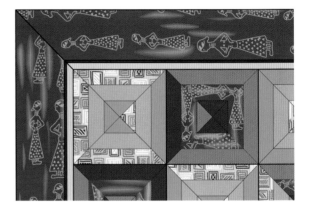

I don't choose the fabric for the border until the center of the quilt is assembled. Then I lay the quilt on the floor and audition fabrics until I'm happy with the results.

WASHING FABRIC

It's wise to wash all fabrics before using them. Some fabrics will shrink, and you'll see immediately if a fabric isn't colorfast. Wash the fabric at the same temperature that you'll use when you wash the finished project.

Strip Piecing

Strip piecing is a fun, easy, and rewarding technique. This section covers all the important aspects of strip piecing. Be sure to read it if you have not made quilts this way before. Accuracy in cutting and piecing is important to the success of your quilts.

EQUIPMENT FOR ROTARY CUTTING

For the strip-piecing techniques used in this book, you'll need a rotary cutter, an 18" x 24" cutting mat, and a 6" x 24" rotary-cutting ruler. Fabric used for patchwork and quilting is 40" to 42" wide. When you fold the fabric in half lengthwise, it will be 20" to 21" wide. You can easily cut the fabric with the 18" x 24" cutting mat and a 24" ruler.

It's important to have a ruler that is printed in two different colors; usually rulers are printed in yellow and black. The black lines will show up on light-colored fabric and the yellow lines will show up on dark colors. For the quilts in this book, you always need a range of hues from light to dark, so a ruler as described above is essential.

When you choose a ruler, be sure that the 45° lines and the 30°/60° lines don't begin in the corner of the ruler. You should always start cutting about ½" before the edge of the fabric begins. When the 45° or 30°/60° lines begin in the corner, there is no space before the fabric to begin cutting with your rotary cutter.

For normal cutting, use the lines and measurements of your ruler; don't use the measurements and lines of your cutting mat for widths less than 6". You can use the lines and measurements of your cutting mat for wide pieces of fabric, but these lines are more for general guidance than for very accurate cutting. When I need to cut pieces wider than my ruler, I prefer to work with two rulers (see "Cutting Square Blocks" on page 10). A 6" x 12" ruler is a very handy size.

It's best if you work on a table that is large enough for you to turn your cutting mat. This avoids having to pick up or disturb your fabrics once you have made a straightening cut along the edge.

CUTTING RELIEF

If you have a lot of cutting to do, try to cut on a high surface. The height of your kitchen counters is good. You won't have to bend as much and you'll prevent back strain.

ROTARY-CUTTING SAFETY

It's important to handle rotary-cutting tools carefully and in the right way. It will lead to better results and prevent injuries. All of the rotary-cutting instructions that follow are written for right-handed quilters. Left-handed quilters should reverse the instructions.

1. Place the ruler on your fabric and apply pressure with the fingertips of your noncutting hand in a spread position and with a straight wrist. Don't press with your hand flat or with a right angle in your wrist. Notice the difference by trying to move the ruler with your free hand. The ruler will move easily when your hand is

flat and less easily when you hold your ruler with your fingertips and with a straight wrist.

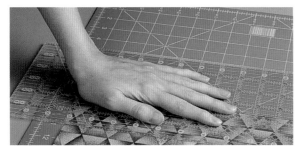

Incorrect

Correct

2. Always place the forefinger of your cutting hand on the rotary cutter as shown. Don't fold all your fingers around the handle of the rotary cutter. With a stretched forefinger you can steer and control the rotary cutter better.

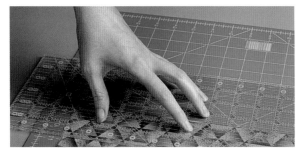

Incorrect

Correct

3. It's very important to always cut at a 90° angle, rolling the rotary cutter directly away from your body. Turn your cutting mat when the fabric and ruler are in a position that makes it impossible to cut away from your body. Cut from about the level of your right hip.

4. Start cutting about ½" *before* the edge of the fabric. To make this possible, make sure that your ruler extends at least 1" beyond the fabric. Roll the rotary cutter blade next to the ruler on the mat. Always close the blade cover immediately after finishing a cut.

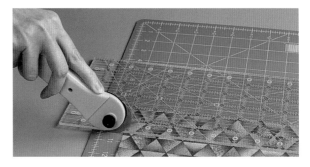

Begin cutting about ½" before the fabric.

CUTTING STRIPS

Before cutting strips, you have to square up the fabric. Don't forget the safety instructions at left when you are cutting.

1. Fold the fabric in half lengthwise, matching the selvages. Place the folded fabric on the cutting mat with the folded edge toward you. Place the ruler on the right side of the fabric. Align a horizontal line on the ruler with the fold so that you will make a straight cut through both layers. Cut away the strip of fabric on the right side of the ruler.

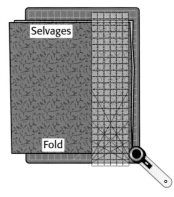

2. Leave the ruler in place on the fabric and fold any fabric extending beyond the cutting mat onto the mat. Turn your mat 180° and unfold the excess fabric.

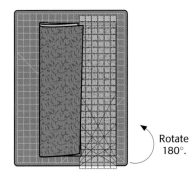

Rotate 180°.

3. Align the ruler with the edge of the fabric at the appropriate ruler marking, and cut your strip.

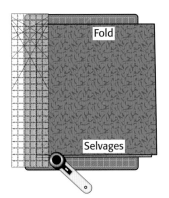

Fold

Selvages

4. After cutting three strips, leave the ruler in place on the fabric, fold the fabric extending beyond the cutting mat onto the mat, and turn the cutting mat 180°. Square up the fabric again as described in step 1. Don't cut more than three strips before squaring up again. When you square up, you'll probably see that the edge doesn't make a 90° angle with the fold anymore. Everyone has a little deviation when cutting, and if you don't adjust it by squaring up again, your strips will have a V at the area where the fold is.

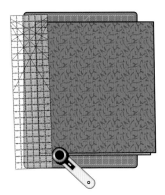

5. After squaring up, rotate the cutting mat 180° and cut three strips again. Turn the cutting mat 180° and square up the fabric again. Repeat the cutting and squaring up until you have cut the number of strips you need.

SEWING STRIP SETS

For all the projects in this book, you'll arrange the strips that you cut in order from light to dark.

1. Take the first and second strip. Align the two strips with right sides together and match the long edges. Sew the strips together with a ¼" seam allowance. Use a short stitch length, about 15 stitches per inch. A shorter stitch helps prevent the seam from coming unsewn when you cut blocks from the strip sets.

SEW STRAIGHT

When you sew strips on your sewing machine, use the walking foot. It will help keep your strips straight and even. Without a walking foot, the fabric on top will feed through the machine just a bit slower than the fabric below. If you don't have a walking foot, pin the strips together as shown below. Place the pins at a right angle with the seam. Remove the pins as you get to them, or sew over them very carefully if you use very fine pins. This will keep the two layers of fabric moving evenly through the machine and will help keep your strip sets straight and accurate.

2. For best results, use your iron to press the seam before opening the fabric; then open the fabric and press again, pressing the seam toward the darker fabric.

3. Take the fourth and the fifth strips and sew them together. Press the seam toward the darker color.

4. Sew the third and sixth strips to the second and fifth strips. Press.

5. If you are making a strip set with six strips, sew the final seam between the third and the fourth strip. Press.

CUTTING BLOCKS FROM STRIP SETS

All the blocks for the quilts in this book are cut from strip sets. Be sure that your strips are carefully pressed before you cut them into blocks. As before, the instructions that follow are written for right-handed quilters. Left-handed quilters will need to reverse the instructions.

Cutting Square Blocks

1. Start by trimming a straight edge on one of the short sides of the strip set. This edge should be cut at a 90º angle to the seams of the strip set. To do this, place the strip set on the cutting mat. Place one of the horizontal lines of the ruler on one of the center seams of the strip set as shown and trim.

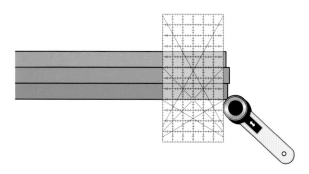

2. Measure the width of the strip set carefully before you cut the squares. If the strip set isn't exactly the expected width, then adapt the measurement before cutting so that you'll cut squares. The measurement of the strip set will determine the measurement of the square to cut. For example, if your strip set measures 4⅞" rather than 5", you'll need to cut 4⅞" squares. Measure all your strip sets before cutting the first one; you must cut all your squares the same.

3. Turn the cutting mat 180°. The just-cut edge is now on the left. Align the appropriate ruler marking on the cut edge and cut your squares.

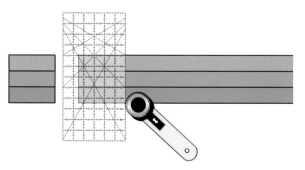

4. Squares up to 6" can be cut with one ruler. For squares from 6" to 12," use two rulers if you don't have a large-enough square ruler. For example, if you need to cut a 9" square, place the 3" ruler marking at the edge of the strip set. Butt a second ruler that is 6" wide against the right edge of the first ruler and cut along the right edge of the second ruler.

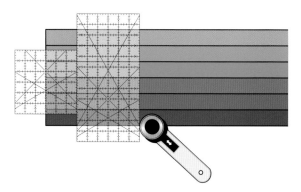

5. Turn the cutting mat 180° when you have cut one square, and square up the strip again. Turn the cutting mat again to cut the next square. It's important to square up the strip set after each cut, because a strip set is seldom really straight.

Cutting 60°-Triangle Blocks

1. Place the strip set on the cutting mat. Place the 60°-angle mark of your ruler on one of the center seams of the strip set at the right end. Trim away the edge.

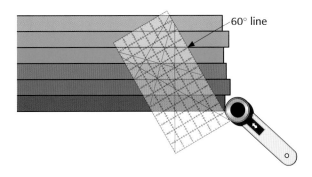

2. Turn the ruler and position it so that the 60°-angle mark lines up with one of the center seams of the strip set and the right edge of the ruler aligns with the upper edge of the previous cut. Cut along the right edge of the ruler. Turn the ruler again to cut a second triangle. Repeat to cut the desired number of triangles.

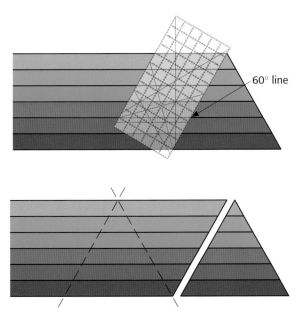

Cutting Quarter-Square-Triangle Blocks

1. Place the strip set on the cutting mat. Place the 45°-angle mark of your ruler on one of the center seams of the strip set at the right end. Trim away the edge.

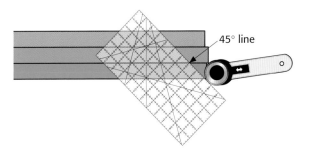

2. Turn the ruler and position it so that the 45°-angle mark lines up with one of the center seams of the strip set and the right edge aligns with the upper edge of the previous cut. Cut along the right edge of the ruler. Turn the ruler again to cut the second triangle. Repeat to cut the desired number of triangles.

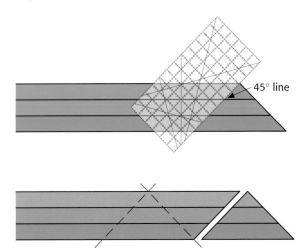

Cutting Oblique-Square Blocks

1. Trim a 90° angle on one of the short sides of the strip set. To do this, place the strip set on the cutting mat. Place one of the horizontal lines of the ruler on one of the center seams of the strip set as shown and trim.

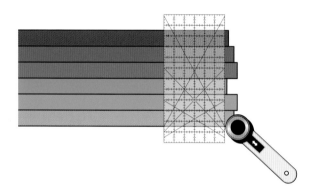

2. Mark a point on the top edge on the right end of the strip as instructed in the directions for the quilt. As an example, we'll use 2½". Align the ruler with this marked point and the lower right corner. Cut along the edge of the ruler.

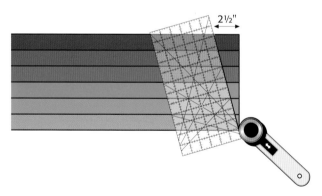

3. Turn the cutting mat 180° and cut the strip set into pieces parallel to the first cutting line. The width of the pieces is provided with the directions for each quilt.

4. Pieces up to a width of 6" can be cut with one ruler. For pieces from 6" to 12", use two rulers if you don't have a large-enough square ruler. When you have to cut an 8"-wide piece, for example, place the 2" line of the first ruler along the edge of the strip set. Butt the second ruler against the right edge of the first ruler and cut along the right edge of the second ruler.

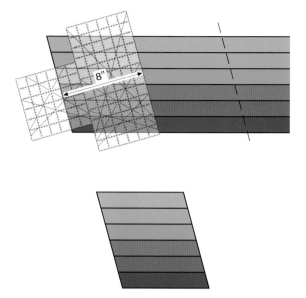

5. Place the piece on the cutting mat with one of the angled-cut edges facing you. Trim the right side to a 90° angle.

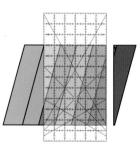

6. Turn the cutting mat 180° and cut a square. Use two rulers when you have to cut squares larger than 6".

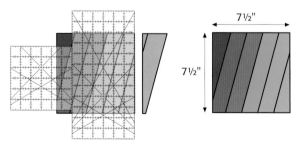

Quilt Construction

Assembling the quilt is the next stage after sewing strip sets and cutting blocks. To complete quilts as quickly and easily as possible, I do everything by machine, including the quilting and binding. But don't rush; take time to enjoy the process and be sure that your quilt is one you'll be proud of. Do the quilting and binding by hand if that is what you prefer.

ARRANGING THE BLOCKS

Take some time to play with the blocks before you sew them together. You can arrange the blocks in many different ways, and perhaps you'll discover a setting that pleases you more than the one I've chosen. Lay the blocks on the floor or on a design wall and arrange them in several ways. Take pictures of the possibilities and compare the differences.

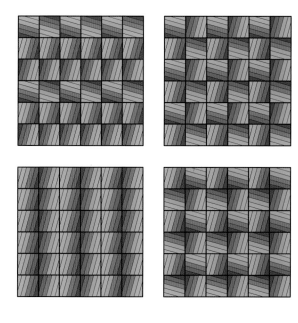

Several quilts in this book are made of the same blocks, but each setting is a different variation. The two crib quilts on pages 21 and 22 are made of exactly the same blocks. "Whirligigs" (page 26) and "Floating Stars" (page 30) are made of the same blocks, but they use different colors and settings, as do "Paapje Strips" (page 58) and "Falling Leaves" (page 62). "Christmas Stars" (page 66) and "The Amazon" (page 70) are made of the same block in different colors, but the angle of the first cut used in each is different. "Breaking Out" (page 50) and "Chateauponsac" (page 46) are made in the same way, but the halves of the blocks are paired and sewn together in different ways, and the settings are quite different.

Look at the quilts and you'll be amazed at the different looks you can achieve with the same basic blocks.

ASSEMBLING STRAIGHT SETS

Arrange the blocks in rows as directed for the specific quilt project, or arrange the blocks in a pattern that pleases you.

1. To sew the blocks into horizontal rows, place the blocks right sides together and align the raw edges. Stitch the seams. Press the seam allowances in opposite directions from row to row. This will keep the intersecting seams neat and flat.

2. Join the rows, matching the seams between the blocks.

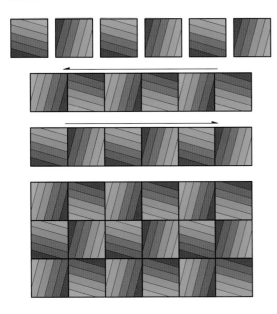

ASSEMBLING TRIANGLE BLOCKS

The quilts in this book that are made from squared blocks in straight settings are sewn together in horizontal rows. The quilts that are made from triangle blocks need to be sewn together in vertical rows.

1. Arrange the blocks as indicated in the directions for each quilt project.

2. To sew the blocks together, you must first sew them in vertical rows. Place the blocks right sides together and align the corners carefully. Stitch the seams. Press the seam allowances to one side or press them open if you need to reduce the bulk of the seam allowances.

3. Join the rows, matching the seams between the blocks. Press the seams open.

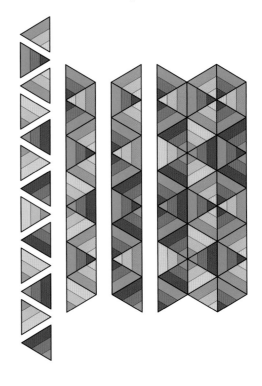

ADDING BORDERS

Most of the quilts in this book have borders with straight-cut corners. Always measure the completed quilt top before you cut the border strips. The measurement of your quilt may deviate from the measurements in this book. The number of strips to cut and the width of the border strips are specified in the directions for each quilt project.

1. Measure the length of the quilt through the center of the quilt. Don't measure along the edges, because they can become slightly stretched from handling.

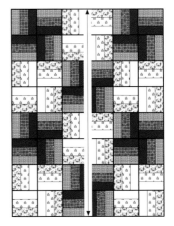

2. Cut two border strips to match the length measurement of the quilt, piecing the strips if necessary.

3. Mark the centers of both sides of the quilt top and the centers of the border strips. Pin the border strips to the quilt top with right sides together, matching the ends and the centers.

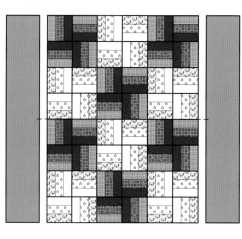

4. Stitch the borders to the quilt top with ¼"-wide seam allowances. Press the seams toward the border strips.

5. Measure the quilt top through the center, including the side borders just added. Cut the top and bottom border strips to the width measured, piecing as necessary. Mark the centers, pin, and stitch the top and bottom borders as you did the side borders. Repeat the process for any additional borders.

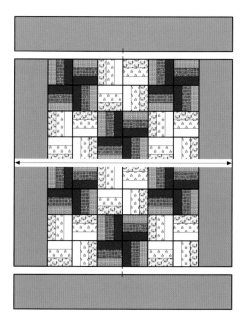

LAYERING AND BASTING

Choose your batting and backing fabric, and then follow the steps below to layer and baste your quilt.

1. Cut the backing fabric and batting 3" or 4" larger than the quilt top all around. For quilts wider than 40", the backing must be pieced. Remove the selvage edges from the fabric and piece the backing with either a horizontal or vertical seam, making the most efficient use of your fabric. Press the seam open to minimize bulk.

2. Lay the backing right side down on a clean, smooth surface, such as a floor or a table. Be sure that the backing is smooth and wrinkle free. Secure the backing with masking tape to the floor or table. Lay the batting on the backing, smoothing out any wrinkles. Then lay the pressed quilt top on the batting.

3. Smooth the quilt top with your hands from the center to the edges. I like to pin the layers together with lots of straight pins before basting. Start pinning in the center and work toward the edges. Remove the masking tape and move the quilt to a table (if it's not already on one) to make it easier on your back.

4. For hand quilting, baste the layers together with needle and thread, making a grid of basting stitches about 4" apart. For machine quilting, I also use thread basting. Of course, your walking foot or darning foot may get tangled in the basting thread, but I always have scissors handy to cut the basting thread if necessary.

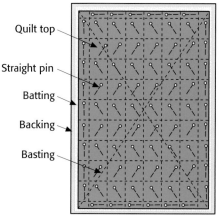

Quilt top
Straight pin
Batting
Backing
Basting

Thread basting

You can also baste with safety pins for machine quilting: place the safety pins 6" to 8" apart, away from the area you intend to quilt. Always baste from the center of the quilt toward the edges. Once you have basted the layers together, remove the straight pins.

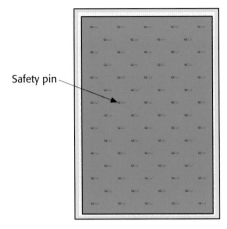

Safety pin

Pin basting

PIECED BATTINGS

It's easy to make a pieced batting if you want to use up smaller pieces left over from other quilt projects. Cut the batting pieces so they butt together and don't lie on top of each other. Whipstitch the pieces together.

MACHINE QUILTING

All the quilts in this book are machine quilted. It's a good method to use with the quick and easy strip-piecing techniques. Your quilt will be sturdy and very usable, and there are many wonderful designs that can be quilted using your machine. Layer and baste the quilt as described in "Layering and Basting" on page 15.

Straight-Line Quilting

For straight-line quilting, use a walking foot on your sewing machine if you have one. A walking foot is very helpful because it allows the layers of the quilt to move through the sewing machine evenly. Always work from the center of the quilt outward. Secure the beginning and ending stitches by changing the stitch length to zero and taking about five stitches in place. Don't sew too fast. When you need to turn a corner, stop with the needle in the down position before raising the presser foot and pivoting.

Free-Motion Quilting

Free-motion quilting allows you to control the direction of the stitching. You can stitch curved designs easily and avoid having to manipulate a large quilt through your sewing machine. Attach a darning foot and lower or cover the feed dogs. The stitch length is determined by the speed at which you run the machine and simultaneously feed the fabric under the darning foot. Try to move your hands slowly and guide the fabric under the needle. Keep the machine running at a consistent speed. Begin and end your stitching by taking a few stitches in place.

Free-motion quilting is a lot like sketching or doodling with your sewing machine. The key is to "draw" with a continuous line—you should not interrupt the line of the design any more than necessary. Try to avoid a lot of starts and stops, and always practice any free-motion stitching before you stitch your quilt.

Stipple quilting, curved quilting lines that meander like puzzle pieces, is a good way to fill a large area, and it's easy to do. Shapes are formed with a continuous motion. The stitching lines should not cross each other or look too uniform. When you are comfortable with stipple quilting, you can try other free-motion quilting designs.

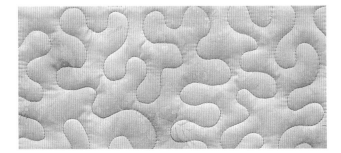

Free-motion quilting without first marking the design is well suited for simple allover designs such as the star design on page 77. In other cases, such as the ivy leaves of "Falling Leaves," you can mark the perimeter of the design and fill in the details without marking them. Notice that I sometimes sew a line twice; I like how this emphasizes the sketching character of the design.

Quilting "Upside Down"

When the quilting design is more complex or more structured, you have to mark the quilt design first. Like many quilters, I don't like to mark on the front side of my quilt. So I mark the designs on the back of the quilt and quilt with the backing up. Let's take a close look at two quilts that are quilted this way.

"Falling Leaves" on page 62 is quilted with a large ivy leaf in a random allover design. For this pattern, the exact placement of the leaves isn't important since the quilting design does not relate directly to the patchwork design.

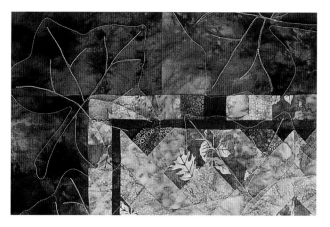

Allover quilting design using an ivy-leaf pattern

In "Breaking Out" on page 50, each block is quilted with a golden spiral. Now, the placement of the design does matter in this case. The spiral design comes from the red fabric used in the quilt. The red fabric is printed with a little golden spiral; this spiral was enlarged and used as the quilting design. In order to know where to mark and quilt the design on the back of the quilt, the front of the quilt is stitched with straight-line quilting around each block first.

Spiral designs quilted in each block and in the border

There's another benefit of this method: metallic threads, such as the gold used in "Breaking Out," are not very strong and will break easily when used as needle thread. By quilting upside down, the gold can be used in the bobbin and a nonmetallic thread can be used in the needle.

The border was quilted with the same spiral design by using bluish green thread that blends with the border fabric. Before the design was marked on the back of "Breaking Out," the center of the quilt was quilted ¹⁄₁₆" outside the center, and the backing and batting were trimmed even with the edges of the quilt top. That allowed the quilter to see where to mark the quilting design.

ADDING A HANGING SLEEVE

To hang a quilt on the wall, you must have a hanging sleeve attached to the back of the quilt to slip a rod through. Use the same fabric as the backing so that it will blend in.

1. Cut a strip of fabric as long as the width of the quilt and about 5" wide for a small quilt or 7" wide for a large one. Hem both short ends of the strip.

2. Fold the strip lengthwise, wrong sides together. Before you attach the binding to the quilt, pin the strip to the back of the quilt, matching the raw edges at the top of the quilt.

Pin sleeve to the top edge of quilt, matching raw edges.

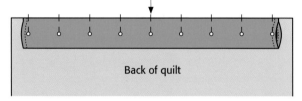

Back of quilt

3. Add the binding to the quilt as directed below, sewing the hanging sleeve in the binding seam. Blindstitch the folded edge of the sleeve to the back of the quilt after the binding has been added.

Blindstitch folded edge in place.

BINDING

All the quilts in this book were bound with double-fold bias binding that finishes at ½". I prefer bias binding because it wears well, and I often use a plaid or checked fabric for binding. I like the look of plaids and checks cut on the bias. In addition, I round the corners on my quilts so that I can sew the binding to the quilt without having to miter the corners. The bias binding strips go around the rounded corners easily.

The yardages in the materials list for each quilt are adequate for cutting either straight-grain or bias strips that are 3" wide. Cut your strips narrower if you prefer a narrower finished binding. If you prefer to miter the corners of your binding, you can cut the strips cross-grain if desired.

Cutting Bias Binding

To cut strips for double-fold bias binding:

1. Fold the fabric for the binding as shown. Pay careful attention to the position of the lettered corners.

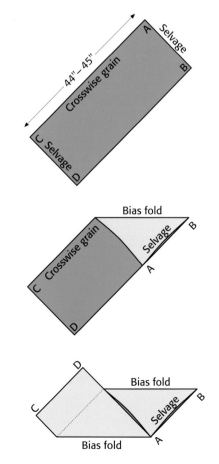

2. Cut the strips 3" wide, cutting perpendicular to the folds as shown by the dashed lines. You'll need enough 3"-wide strips to go around the perimeter of the quilt plus 10" for seams.

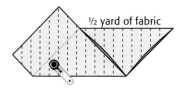

½ yard of fabric

Attaching the Binding

To attach the binding:

1. Trim the batting and backing ¼" beyond the edges of the quilt top so that the 3"-wide binding will be filled out nicely. To make slightly rounded corners, place the edge of a teacup on each quilt corner and draw around the curve from one side of the quilt to the other. Cut on the drawn line.

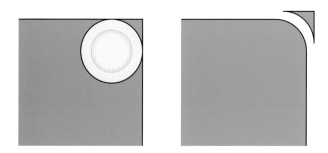

2. Join the binding strips, right sides together, with a ¼" seam allowance to make one long piece of binding. Press the seams open.

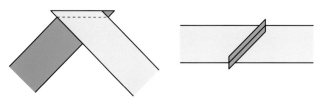

3. Fold the binding lengthwise, wrong sides together, and press.

4. Working from the back of the quilt, align the raw edges of the binding ¼" away from the raw edge of the backing. Leaving the first 10" of the binding unsewn, stitch the binding in place with a ¼" seam allowance.

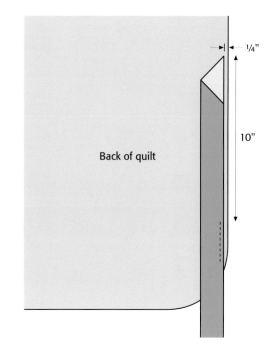

¼"

10"

Back of quilt

5. As you approach a corner, pin the binding around the curve before you sew. Gently ease the binding around the curve. Don't stretch the binding as you pin it in position. If the binding is stretched, the corner won't lie flat.

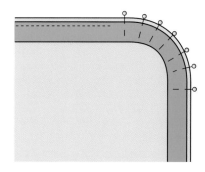

6. Sew carefully around the corner, gently easing the binding around the curve. Remove the pins as you get to them, or sew over them very carefully. Continue sewing around the edges of the quilt, pinning and easing the binding around the remaining corners as you get to them.

7. When you are within 10" of the starting point, remove the quilt from the sewing machine and lay the quilt on a flat surface. Fold the unsewn binding ends back on themselves so that they just meet in the middle over the unsewn area of the quilt. Finger-press or pin both binding ends to mark this junction.

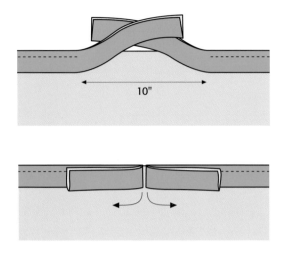

8. Unfold both ends of the binding. With right sides together, match the pressed lines, having the binding strips open and at a right angle to each other. Sew across the intersection on the diagonal. Trim the excess fabric and press the seam open. Finish stitching the binding to the quilt edge.

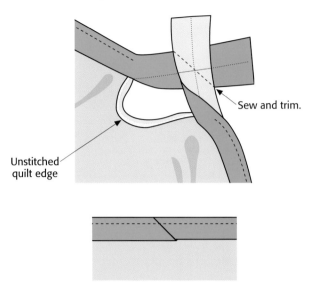

9. Fold the binding over the raw edges to the front of the quilt. Stitch in place by machine with the folded edge covering the first row of machine stitching.

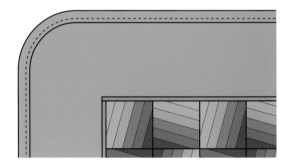

Crib Quilts in Blue and White

Crib Quilt 1 by Maaike Bakker, 2003

This simple pieced design lends itself to many fabric combinations, whether they're sophisticated prints, such as these Dutch and German fabrics, or fun juvenile prints. The quilting in the border adds a very special touch to this sweet baby quilt and can be the inspiration for stories to tell the child who sleeps under it.

Finished quilt: 40" x 49" ❋ Finished block: 4½"

Crib Quilt 2 by Maaike Bakker, 2003

I used the same blocks as in "Crib Quilt 1," but arranged them in a different way. The Rail Fence blocks can be set in a variety of ways to achieve different looks. The light-to-dark fabric arrangement adds dimension to the simple block pattern.

Finished quilt: 41" x 50" ❀ **Finished block:** 4½"

MATERIALS

Yardage is based on 42"-wide fabric.

Fabric	Crib Quilt 1	Crib Quilt 2
6 different fabrics in gradations from white to dark blue for blocks	¼ yard of *each*	⅜ yard of *each*
Solid dark blue for borders	⅞ yard	1⅛ yards
Blue-and-white plaid for binding	⅝ yard	⅝ yard
Fabric for backing	2⅝ yards	2⅝ yards
Batting	46" x 55" piece	47" x 56" piece

CUTTING

All measurements include ¼" seam allowances. Before you cut, read "Cutting Strips" on page 8.

Fabric	Crib Quilt 1	Crib Quilt 2
6 fabrics for blocks	3 strips from *each*, 2" x 42"	4 strips from *each*, 2" x 42"
Solid dark blue	4 strips, 6½" x 42"	4 strips, 1¾" x 42"
		4 strips, 5" x 42"
Blue-and-white plaid	3"-wide bias strips to total 190"	3"-wide bias strips to total 194"

MAKING THE BLOCKS

Refer to "Sewing Strip Sets" on page 9 and "Cutting Square Blocks" on page 10.

1. Arrange the six different white to dark blue strips from light to dark. Sew the strips into two sets of three strips each as shown. Press the seams in one direction, toward the darker colors. Make three strip sets of each combination. (If you are making

"Crib Quilt 2," you will have six strips left over; set these aside for the border.)

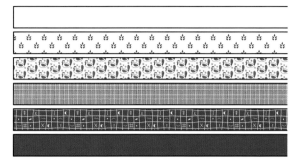

Arrange strips from light to dark.

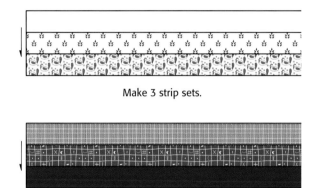

Make 3 strip sets.

Make 3 strip sets.

2. Trim one of the short sides of each strip set to a 90º angle. Measure the width of the strip sets carefully before you cut. If your strip sets are not 5" wide, adjust the measurements to cut squares that are equal to the width of your strip sets. Cut the six strip sets into squares. Each strip set will yield 8 squares, for a total of 48 (24 of each color combination).

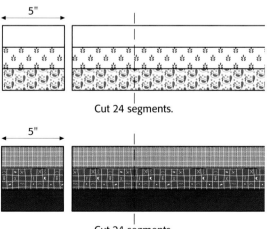

Cut 24 segments.

Cut 24 segments.

ASSEMBLING THE QUILT TOP

1. Arrange the blocks in one of the settings shown. Or play with the blocks on a design wall to determine a setting that you like, referring to "Arranging the Blocks" on page 13. You'll have eight rows of six blocks each.

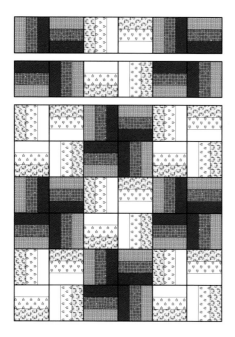

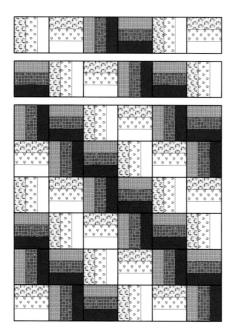

2. Sew the blocks together in horizontal rows. Press the seams in opposite direction from row to row. Join the rows.

3. Refer to "Adding Borders" on page 14. Measure the quilt through the center before cutting the borders. There are two different borders used for these two crib quilts: a single, plain border if you are making "Crib Quilt 1" or multiple borders, including a pieced border, if you are making "Crib Quilt 2."

MAKING THE PLAIN BORDER: CRIB QUILT 1

1. Measure the length of the quilt through the center and cut two of the 6½"-wide solid dark blue strips to fit the length of the quilt. Sew the border strips to the sides of the quilt top and press the seams toward the borders.

2. Measure the width of the quilt through the center, including the just-added borders. Cut and sew the remaining two 6½"-wide border strips to the top and bottom of the quilt. Press.

MAKING MULTIPLE BORDERS: CRIB QUILT 2

1. Arrange the remaining six white to dark blue strips from light to dark. Sew them together into one strip set. Press toward the darker fabrics. Cut 18 segments, 1¼" wide.

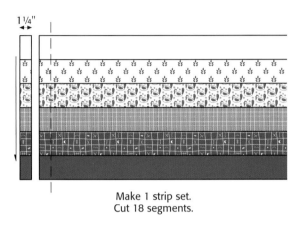

1¼"

Make 1 strip set.
Cut 18 segments.

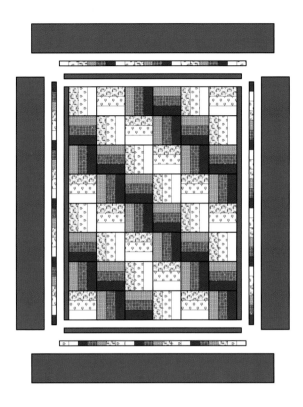

2. Sew the segments together, end to end, into one long strip. Set the strip aside.

3. Measure the length of the quilt through the center and cut two of the 1¾"-wide solid dark blue strips to this length. Sew them to the sides of the quilt. Press the seams toward the border strips.

4. Measure the width of the quilt through the center, including the just-added borders. Cut and sew the remaining two 1¾"-wide strips to the top and bottom. Press.

5. Repeat the measuring, cutting, and sewing procedure to add the pieced border strips to the quilt. Press the seams toward the solid border strips.

6. Repeat to add the 5"-wide solid dark blue border strips to the quilt. Press the seams toward the solid border.

FINISHING THE QUILT

1. Layer the quilt top with batting and backing; baste.

2. Machine quilt the center of the quilt with variegated thread in a large stipple or meandering design.

3. Quilt the outer borders with free-motion designs. I used houses, flowers, trees, cars, and a church on "Crib Quilt 1." These designs are on page 76. For "Crib Quilt 2," quilt the narrow borders ⅟₁₆" outside each border. Quilt the outer border using the hearts pattern on page 77.

4. Attach a hanging sleeve, if desired, referring to "Adding a Hanging Sleeve" on page 18.

5. Use the blue-and-white plaid strips to bind the edges of the quilt. Refer to "Binding" on page 18.

Whirligigs

Designed by Maaike Bakker and made by Joke Griffioen, 2004

Yellow and purple, used here in this vibrant quilt, are complementary colors—they are opposite of each other on the color wheel. When you arrange these colors in a tonal scale, yellow will be the lightest and purple the darkest.

Finished quilt: 57½" x 69" ❋ **Finished block:** 5" equilateral triangle

MATERIALS

Yardage is based on 42"-wide fabric.

¾ yard *each* of 6 colors ranging from yellow to red to purple for blocks

1⅞ yards of orange plaid for the outer border and bias binding

½ yard of solid burgundy fabric for the inner border

3⅝ yards of fabric for the backing

64" x 75" piece of batting

CUTTING

All measurements include ¼" seam allowances. Before you cut, read "Cutting Strips" on page 8.

From *each* of the 6 colors ranging from yellow to purple, cut:

❋ 10 strips, 2" x 42"

From the solid burgundy fabric, cut:

❋ 6 strips, 2" x 42"

From the orange plaid, cut:

❋ 7 strips, 5½" x 42"
❋ 3"-wide bias strips to total 265"

MAKING THE BLOCKS

Refer to "Sewing Strip Sets" on page 9 and "Cutting 60°-Triangle Blocks" on page 11.

1. Arrange the six different yellow to purple strips from light to dark. Sew the strips into two sets of three strips each as shown. Press the seams in one direction, toward the darker colors. Make 10 strip sets of each combination.

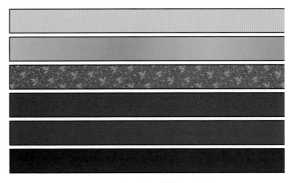

Arrange strips from light to dark.

Make 10 strip sets.

Make 10 strip sets.

2. Place the 60°-angle mark of a ruler on one of the inner seams of a strip set and cut a 60° angle. Reverse the direction of the ruler to cut a second

60° angle. Continue in this manner and cut each strip set into 12 equilateral triangles.

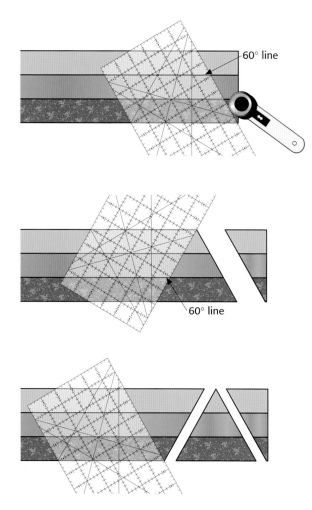

3. You'll have four different equilateral-triangle blocks. Stack like triangles together. You'll have 240 triangles total—60 of each kind. For the quilt shown, you need 230 triangles, so 10 are extra.

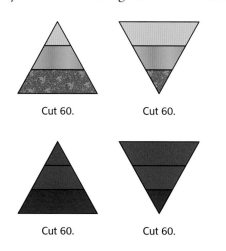

Cut 60. Cut 60.

Cut 60. Cut 60.

ASSEMBLING THE QUILT TOP

1. Arrange the blocks as shown, or play with the blocks on a design wall to determine a setting that you like. See "Arranging the Blocks" on page 13.

2. Sew the blocks together in vertical rows, pressing the seams to one side or open to minimize bulk. Join the rows and press.

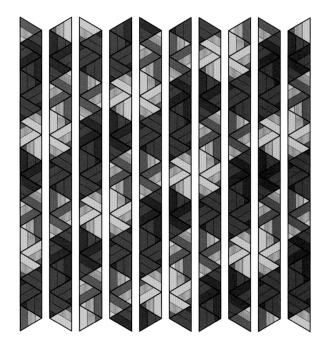

3. Trim the top and bottom of the quilt top with a rotary cutter and ruler, leaving ¼" for seam allowances.

4. Refer to "Adding Borders" on page 14. Measure the length of the quilt through the center. Sew the 2"-wide burgundy strips together end to end into one long strip and cut two side border strips as measured. Sew the strips to the sides of the quilt and press the seams toward the borders.

5. Measure the width of the quilt through the center, including the borders just added. Cut and sew 2"-wide burgundy strips to the top and bottom of the quilt. Press.

6. Repeat the measuring, cutting, and sewing procedure to add the 5½"-wide orange plaid border strips to the quilt. Press the seams toward the outer border.

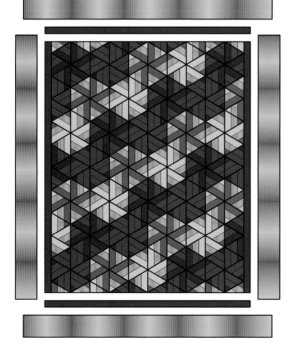

Note that the seams of the blocks do not align or match up. Don't worry; it's not a mistake. Your quilt will resemble the quilt in the photograph.

Finishing the Quilt

1. Layer the quilt top with batting and backing; baste.

2. Quilt the pinwheels ⅟₁₆" inside the seam line as shown. Quilt the inner border ⅟₁₆" inside the border. For the border design, make a template by tracing one half of the pinwheel blades. Quilt the outer border with half pinwheels by drawing the pattern on the backing of the border and stitching on the marked lines. Refer to "Quilting 'Upside Down'" on page 17.

3. Attach a hanging sleeve, if desired, referring to "Adding a Hanging Sleeve" on page 18.

4. Use the orange plaid strips to bind the edges of the quilt. Refer to "Binding" on page 18.

Floating Stars

By Maaike Bakker and Elly Weteling, 2004

This quilt uses the same blocks as "Whirligigs" on page 26, but in different colors. It's amazing how different the two quilts look with just a slightly different arrangement of the blocks.

Finished quilt: 42½" x 49½" ✿ **Finished block:** 4⅜" equilateral triangle

MATERIALS

Yardage is based on 42"-wide fabric.

⅜ yard *each* of 6 colors ranging from yellow to green to blue for blocks

⅞ yard of bright green print for outer border

¼ yard of dark green for inner border

⅝ yard of green plaid fabric for binding

2¾ yards of fabric for backing

49" x 56" piece of batting

3 blue buttons, ¾" diameter

22 yellow buttons, ½" diameter

CUTTING

All measurements include ¼" seam allowances. Before you cut, read "Cutting Strips" on page 8.

From *each* of the 6 colors ranging from yellow to blue, cut:

❀ 6 strips, 1¾" x 42"

From the dark green, cut:

❀ 4 strips, 1¼" x 42"

From the bright green, cut:

❀ 4 strips, 5½" x 42"

From the green plaid, cut:

❀ 3"-wide bias strips to total 196"

MAKING THE BLOCKS

Refer to "Sewing Strip Sets" on page 9 and "Cutting 60°-Triangle Blocks" on page 11.

1. Arrange the six different yellow to blue strips from light to dark. Sew the three lighter strips together and the three darker strips together as shown to make two strip sets. Press the seams toward the darker colors. Make six strip sets of each combination.

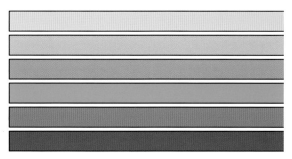

Arrange strips from light to dark.

Make 6 strip sets.

Make 6 strip sets.

2. Place the 60°-angle mark of a ruler on one of the inner seams of a strip set and cut a 60° angle. Reverse the direction of the ruler to cut a second 60° angle, but slide the ruler ¼" along the top of the strip set. This will prevent the top triangle

from being too small in the finished block. Continue in this manner and cut each strip set into 14 equilateral triangles.

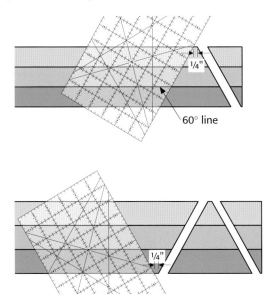

3. You'll have 4 different equilateral-triangle blocks, 42 of each, for a total of 168. Stack like triangles together. You need 144 for the quilt top; 24 will be extra.

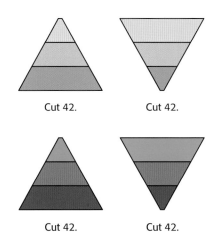

Cut 42.   Cut 42.

Cut 42.   Cut 42.

ASSEMBLING THE QUILT TOP

1. Arrange the blocks as shown, or play with the blocks on a design wall to determine a setting that you like. See "Arranging the Blocks" on page 13.

2. Sew the blocks together in vertical rows. Press the seams open so that the blocks will be flatter. Join the rows and press seams open.

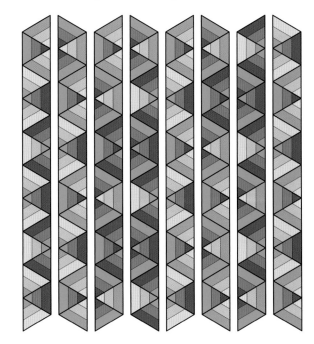

3. Trim the top and bottom of the quilt top with a rotary cutter and ruler, leaving ¼" for seam allowances.

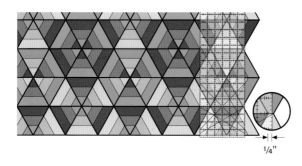

4. Refer to "Adding Borders" on page 14. Measure the quilt before cutting border strips. Measure the length of the quilt through the center and cut the 1¼"-wide dark green strips to fit the length of the quilt. Sew the strips to opposite sides of the quilt top and press the seams toward the borders.

5. Measure the width of the quilt through the center, including the borders just added. Cut and sew the 1¼"-wide dark green strips to the top and bottom of the quilt. Press.

6. Repeat the measuring, cutting, and sewing procedure to add the 5½"-wide bright green border strips to the quilt. Press the seams toward the bright green border.

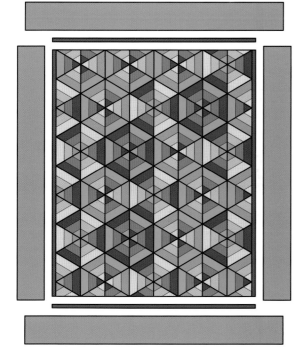

FINISHING THE QUILT

1. Layer the quilt top with batting and backing; baste.

2. Quilt the three large blue stars ⅛" outside the edges. Quilt the hexagons inside each blue star ⅛" outside the edges. Quilt the dark green inner border ⅛" outside the center of the quilt and ⅛" outside the border. Make a template of a 60° triangle with 4" sides and draw a garland of dancing triangles on the backing in the border area; quilt the marked design. Refer to "Quilting 'Upside Down'" on page 17.

3. Sew a blue button in the center of each blue star. Sew the small yellow buttons at the intersections of unquilted triangles.

4. Attach a hanging sleeve, if desired, referring to "Adding a Hanging Sleeve" on page 18.

5. Use the green plaid strips to bind the edges of the quilt. Refer to "Binding" on page 18.

Women of Africa

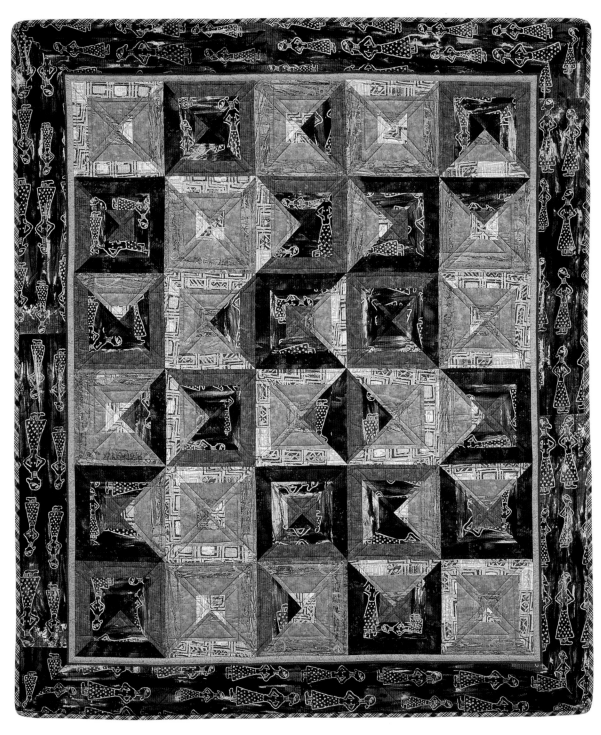

By Maaike Bakker, 2004

Fabrics from Africa in earthy tones give this quilt a warm glow; the gold printed designs add depth and richness. Here's an opportunity to use a special collection of fabrics.

Finished quilt: 66" x 76¼" ✳ **Finished block:** 10⅜"

MATERIALS

Yardage is based on 42"-wide fabric.

⅞ yard *each* of 6 colors ranging from yellow to gold to dark brown for blocks

1⅜ yards of brown print for outer border

⅜ yard of light pink for inner border

¼ yard of bright pink for middle border

¾ yard of brown plaid for binding

4⅝ yards of fabric for backing

72" x 83" piece of batting

CUTTING

All measurements include ¼" seam allowances. Before you cut, read "Cutting Strips" on page 8.

From *each* of the 6 colors ranging from yellow to dark brown, cut:

❀ 10 strips, 2¼" x 42"

From the light pink, cut:

❀ 6 strips, 1¼" x 42"

From the bright pink, cut:

❀ 7 strips, ¾" x 42"

From the brown print, cut:

❀ 8 strips, 6" x 42"

From the brown plaid, cut:

❀ 3"-wide bias strips to total 297"

MAKING THE BLOCKS

Refer to "Sewing Strip Sets" on page 9 and "Cutting Quarter-Square-Triangle Blocks" on page 11.

1. Arrange the six different yellow to brown strips from light to dark. Sew the three lighter strips

together and the three darker strips together as shown to make 2 strip sets. Press the seams toward the darker colors. Make 10 strip sets of each combination.

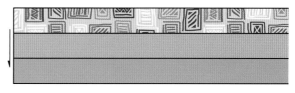

Make 10 strip sets.

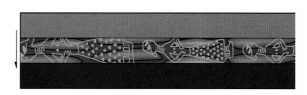

Make 10 strip sets.

2. Place the 45°-angle mark of a ruler on one of the inner seams of a strip set and cut a 45° angle. Reverse the direction of the ruler to cut a second 45° angle. Continue in this manner and cut each strip set into six quarter-square triangles.

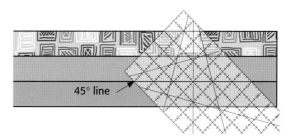

45° line

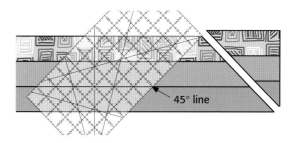

45° line

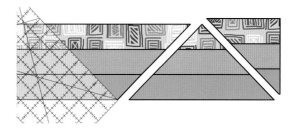

3. You'll have 4 different triangles, 30 of each, for a total of 120. Stack like triangles together.

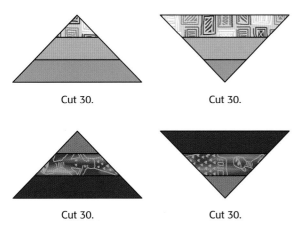

Cut 30.   Cut 30.

Cut 30.   Cut 30.

4. Use three of the same triangles from one stack and one triangle from a different stack. Sew the four triangles together to make a block. Press the seams open. Continue to combine triangles in the same manner to make 30 blocks.

Make a total of 30 blocks.

Assembling the Quilt Top

1. Arrange the blocks as shown, or play with the blocks on a design wall to determine a setting that you like. See "Arranging the Blocks" on page 13.

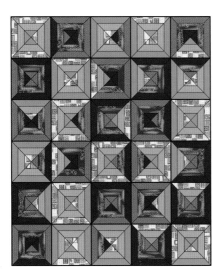

2. Sew the blocks into horizontal rows and then join the rows.

3. This quilt has mitered borders. To make mitered borders, sew the border strips together and treat them as one unit. Sew the 1¼"-wide light pink strips together end to end to make one long strip; then cut this strip into two strips that are 57" long and two strips that are 67" long.

4. Sew the ¾"-wide bright pink strips together to make a long strip; then cut this into two strips that are 60" long and two strips that are 70" long.

5. Sew the brown print strips together in pairs to make four long strips. Cut two to a length of 70" and leave the other two (which should be at least 80" long) as they are.

6. Sew a 57" light pink strip, a 60" bright pink strip, and a 70" brown print strip together, matching the centers. Make two for the top and bottom borders.

Center

Make 2.

7. Sew a 67" light pink strip, a 70" bright pink strip, and a long brown print strip together, matching the centers. Make two for the side borders.

8. Fold the quilt top in half and mark the center of the quilt edges. Fold each border strip in half and mark the center with a pin.

9. Measure the length and width of the quilt top across the center. Note the measurements.

10. Place a pin at each end of the side border strips to mark the length of the quilt top. Repeat with the top and bottom borders.

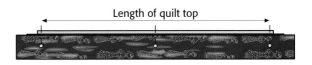

Length of quilt top

11. With right sides together, pin the borders to the quilt top, matching the centers. Line up the pins at each end of the border strip with the edges of the quilt. Sew the borders to the quilt top, beginning and ending the stitching ¼" from the raw edges of the quilt top. Backstitch at each end to secure the seam.

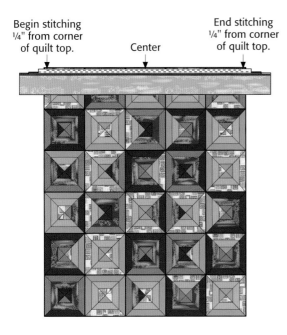

Begin stitching ¼" from corner of quilt top.   Center   End stitching ¼" from corner of quilt top.

12. For one corner, fold the quilt top diagonally with wrong sides together so that the border strips are aligned with right sides together. Use a ruler to draw a line at a 45° angle from the end of the stitched line to the outside edge.

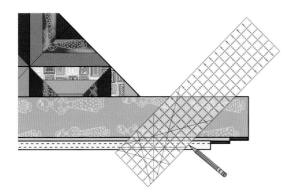

13. Stitch on the drawn line. Trim the excess fabric to ¼" from the seam. Press the seam allowance open.

14. Repeat steps 12 and 13 for the remaining corners.

FINISHING THE QUILT

1. Layer the quilt top with batting and backing; baste.

2. Quilt the light pink inner border ⅟₁₆" inside the center of the quilt. Quilt the bright pink border ⅟₁₆" outside both edges. Quilt the center of the quilt and the outer border as shown, using a walking foot.

3. Attach a hanging sleeve, if desired, referring to "Adding a Hanging Sleeve" on page 18.

4. Use the brown plaid strips to bind the edges of the quilt. Refer to "Binding" on page 18.

Good Night

By Maaike Bakker and Tineke Zweers, 2005

*This simple but surprising pattern makes a friendly and fun quilt
for a child. It can also be a striking wall hanging.*

Finished quilt: 46½" x 63½" ❀ **Finished block:** 4¼"

MATERIALS

Yardage is based on 42"-wide fabric.

¾ yard *each* of 5 blue prints in gradations from light to dark for the blocks

1⅛ yards of dark blue print for inner and outer border

⅞ yard of yellow print for stars and middle border

⅝ yard of blue plaid for binding

3 yards of fabric for backing

52" x 69" piece of batting

CUTTING

All measurements include ¼" seam allowances. Before you cut, read "Cutting Strips" on page 8.

From *each* of the 5 blue prints, cut:

❀ 7 strips, 2½" x 42"

From the yellow print, cut:

❀ 7 strips, 2½" x 42"

❀ 5 strips, 1" x 42"

From the dark blue print, cut:

❀ 5 strips, 1½" x 42"

❀ 6 strips, 4¾" x 42"

From the blue plaid, cut:

❀ 3"-wide bias strips to total 232"

MAKING THE BLOCKS

Refer to "Sewing Strip Sets" on page 9 and "Cutting Oblique-Square Blocks" on page 12.

1. Arrange the five different blue strips from light to dark. Place a 2½" yellow strip in the top position as shown. Sew the top three strips together and the bottom three strips together to make two strip sets. Press the seams toward the darker colors. Make seven strip sets of each combination.

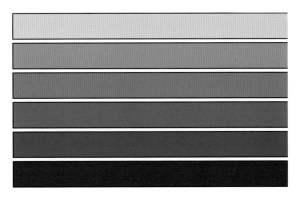

Arrange strips from light to dark.

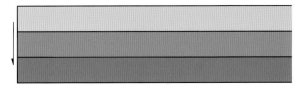

Make 7 strip sets.

Make 7 strip sets.

2. Place the strip sets on the cutting mat with the yellow strip on top and the darkest blue strip on top. Trim one of the short sides of a strip set at a 90º angle. Mark a point about 3" from the end on the top side of the strip set. Place a ruler at the bottom-right corner and line it up with the 3" mark at the top. Cut along the ruler from the lower-right corner to the marked point at the top.

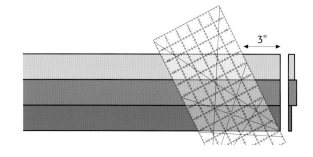

3. Rotate the cutting mat so that the cut end of the strip set is on the left and cut the strip set into 7 segments, 4¾" wide and parallel to the first cutting line. Repeat for the other strip sets. Note: If you cannot cut 7 segments from your strip set, there is enough fabric to make another strip set of each combination. Cut 6 or 7 segments from each strip set for a total of 98 segments.

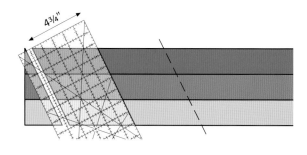

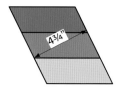

Cut 7 from each strip set.

4. Cut these segments into 4¾" squares. You'll have 2 different blocks, 49 of each and 98 total. Two are extra.

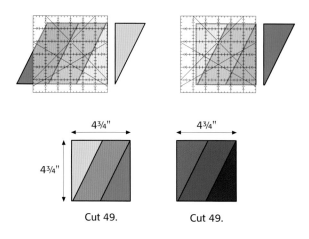

4¾"   4¾"

4¾"

Cut 49.   Cut 49.

ASSEMBLING THE QUILT TOP

1. Arrange the blocks as shown, or play with the blocks on a design wall to determine a setting that you like. See "Arranging the Blocks" on page 13. Sew the blocks together in 12 horizontal rows of eight blocks each. Press the seams in opposite directions from row to row. Join the rows.

2. Refer to "Adding Borders" on page 14. Measure the length of the quilt through the center. Sew three 1½"-wide dark blue strips together end to end into one long strip and cut the strip into two borders to fit the quilt. Sew the strips to the sides of the quilt and press the seams toward the borders.

3. Measure the width of the quilt through the center, including the borders just added. Trim and sew the remaining 1½"-wide dark blue strips to the top and bottom of the quilt. Press.

4. Repeat the measuring, cutting, and sewing procedure to add the 1"-wide yellow border strips.

5. Repeat to add the 4¾"-wide dark blue strips.

FINISHING THE QUILT

1. Layer the quilt with batting and backing; baste.

2. Outline quilt the yellow stars and the yellow border. Fill the background with stipple quilting. Quilt the outer border with the free-motion star design on page 77.

3. Attach a hanging sleeve, if desired, referring to "Adding a Hanging Sleeve" on page 18.

4. Use the blue plaid strips to bind the edges of the quilt. Refer to "Binding" on page 18.

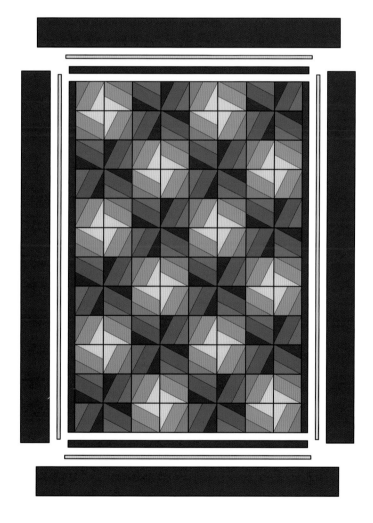

Quilt for Johanna

By Anja Jalving and Aletta Kwant, 2003

Johanna is a niece of Anja and Aletta, two of my students. Johanna was 15 years old when the quilt was made. She chose the fabrics for the quilt by herself, and she wasn't satisfied until she found a red fabric printed with a little gold to fit into the color scheme of her bedroom.

Finished quilt: 67½" x 94" ❄ **Finished block: 7½"**

MATERIALS

Yardage is based on 42"-wide fabric.

1 yard *each* of 6 colors ranging from pink to red to purple for blocks

1½ yards of pink-and-purple print for outer border

¾ yard of solid purple fabric for borders

⅞ yard of dark pink print for binding

6 yards of fabric for backing

74" x 100" piece of batting

CUTTING

All measurements include ¼" seam allowances. Before you cut, read "Cutting Strips" on page 8.

From *each* of the 6 colors ranging from pink to purple, cut:

❀ 18 strips, 1¾" x 42"

From the solid purple fabric, cut:

❀ 3 strips, 1¼" x 42"

❀ 7 strips, 2½" x 42"

From the pink-and-purple print, cut:

❀ 8 strips, 5½" x 42"

From the dark pink print, cut:

❀ 3"-wide bias strips to total 335"

MAKING THE BLOCKS

Refer to "Sewing Strip Sets" on page 9 and "Cutting Square Blocks" on page 10.

1. Arrange the six different pink to purple strips from light to dark. Sew the strips into a strip set as shown. Press the seams toward the darker colors. Make 18 strip sets.

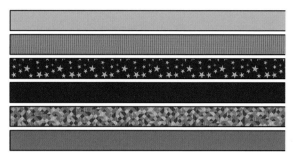

Arrange strips from light to dark.

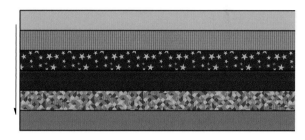

Make 18 strip sets.

2. Trim one of the short sides of each strip set to a 90° angle. Measure the width of the strip sets carefully before you cut squares. If your strip sets are not 8" wide, adjust the measurements to cut squares that are equal to the width of your strip sets. Cut each strip set into 4 squares until you have a total of 70 squares.

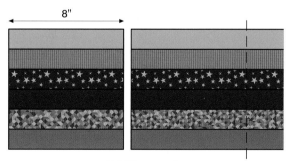

8"

Cut 70 segments.

MAKING THE STRIP-PIECED BORDER

1. Cut the leftovers from the strip sets into 1¾"-wide segments. You need 14 segments.

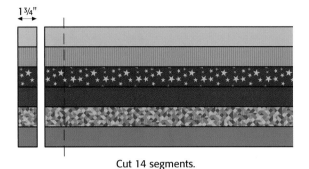

1¾"

Cut 14 segments.

2. For the top border, sew seven segments into a long strip. Repeat to make the bottom border.

Make 2.

ASSEMBLING THE QUILT TOP

1. Arrange the blocks as shown, or play with the blocks on a design wall to determine a setting that you like. See "Arranging the Blocks" on page 13.

   Sew the blocks together in 10 horizontal rows of seven blocks each. Press the seams in opposite directions from row to row. Join the rows. Press the seams in one direction.

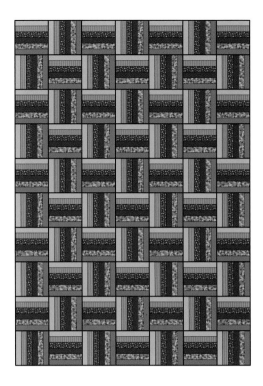

2. Refer to "Adding Borders" on page 14. Measure the width of the quilt through the center. Sew the 1¼"-wide solid purple strips together end to end into one long strip and cut the strip into two borders to fit the quilt. Sew the strips to the top and bottom of the quilt and press the seams toward the borders.

3. Repeat to add the strip-pieced borders to the top and bottom edges of the quilt. Press the seams toward the solid purple strips.

4. Sew the seven 2½"-wide solid purple strips together end to end into a long strip. Measure the width of the quilt through the center. Cut and sew the purple border strips to the top and bottom of the quilt. Press toward the purple strips.

5. Repeat the measuring and sewing procedure to add 2½"-wide purple strips to the sides of the quilt.

6. Sew the 5½"-wide pink-and-purple print strips together end to end into one long strip. Measure the width of the quilt through the center. Cut and sew the strips to the top and bottom of the quilt. Press the seams toward the outer border. Repeat to add the side border strips. Press.

FINISHING THE QUILT

1. Layer the quilt top with batting and backing; baste.

2. Outline quilt the pink zigzag lines that meander over the quilt. Quilt the space between these zig-zag lines with the free-motion star design on page 77. Use the same design to quilt the outer border. Outline quilt the strip-pieced border and the solid purple border.

3. Attach a hanging sleeve, if desired, referring to "Adding a Hanging Sleeve" on page 18.

4. Use the dark pink print strips to bind the edges of the quilt. Refer to "Binding" on page 18.

Chateauponsac

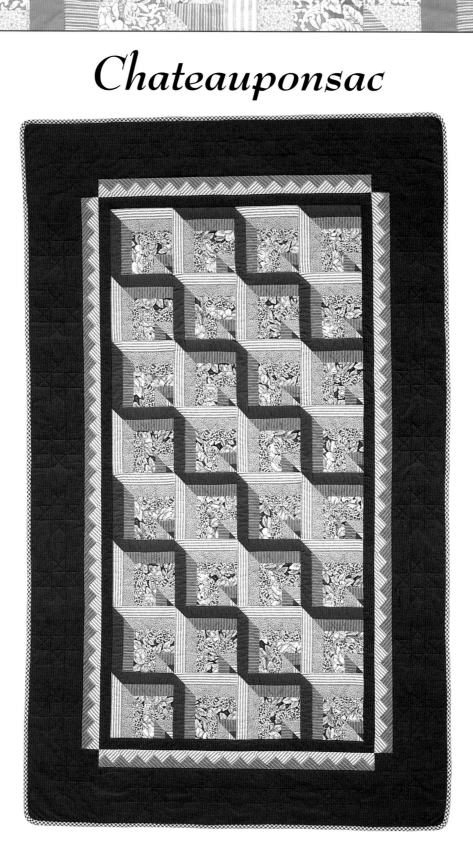

By Maaike Bakker, 2000

Chateauponsac is a beautiful, small medieval town in France. I made this quilt when I was teaching a strip-piecing course there. The quilt serves as a souvenir with many fond memories from a very special week.

Finished quilt: 56½" x 91" ❀ Finished block: 8⅝"

MATERIALS

Yardage is based on 42"-wide fabric.

⅝ yard *each* of 6 blue fabrics in gradations from light to dark for blocks*

2⅛ yards of solid dark blue fabric for borders

⅝ yard *each* of 2 blue fabrics for the strip-pieced border (choose 2 of the 6 block fabrics)*

¾ yard of blue checked fabric for binding

5⅜ yards of fabric for backing

62" x 96" piece of batting

If you want to use a stripe and cut it lengthwise, as I did for the lightest fabric in the blocks, you'll need 1¼ yards of the striped fabric. Be sure to cut it on the lengthwise grain. For the pieced border, I chose to cut a darker stripe lengthwise and the lighter stripe crosswise.

CUTTING

All measurements include ¼" seam allowances. Before you cut, read "Cutting Strips" on page 8.

From *each* of the 6 blue fabrics, cut:

❊ 8 strips, 2" x 42"

From *each* of the 2 blue fabrics for the strip-pieced border, cut:

❊ 6 strips, 3" x 42"

From the solid dark blue fabric, cut:

❊ 6 strips, 2" x 42"

❊ 4 squares, 2½" x 2½"

❊ 7 strips, 7½" x 42"

From the blue checked fabric, cut:

❊ 3"-wide bias strips to total 307"

MAKING THE BLOCKS

Refer to "Sewing Strip Sets" on page 9 and "Cutting Square Blocks" on page 10.

1. Arrange the six different blue strips from light to dark. Sew the strips into a strip set as shown. Press the seams toward the darker blues. Make eight strip sets.

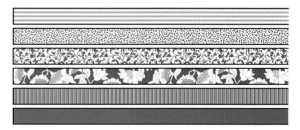

Arrange strips from light to dark.

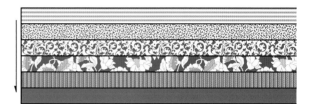

Make 8 strip sets.

2. Trim one of the short sides of each strip set to a 90° angle. Before you cut the squares, measure the width of the strip sets carefully. If your strip sets are not 9½" wide, adjust the measurements to cut squares that are equal to the width of your strip sets. Cut each strip set into 4 squares for a total of 32 squares.

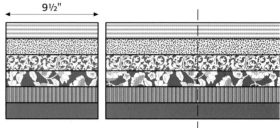

9½"

Cut 32 segments.

3. Cut 16 of the squares in half diagonally with the ruler going from the top right to the bottom left. Reverse the cutting direction for the remaining blocks. You'll have four different triangles, 16 of each. Label them and stack like triangles together.

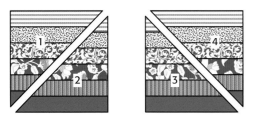

Cut 16 of each.

4. Make 16 blocks using triangles 1 and 3 and make 16 blocks using triangles 2 and 4. The blocks should measure 9⅛" x 9⅛".

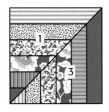 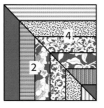

Make 16.   Make 16.

MAKING THE STRIP-PIECED BORDER

1. Sew the 3"-wide blue strips together in pairs. Press the seams toward the darker color.

2. Trim one of the short sides of each strip set to a 90° angle. Cut the strip sets into 120 segments, 2" wide.

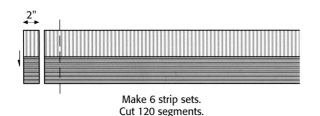

Make 6 strip sets.
Cut 120 segments.

3. Sew the segments together as shown, offsetting them by 1⅜". Press the seams open or all in one direction. Make two strips with 20 segments each and two strips with 36 segments each.

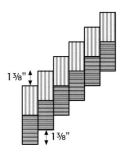

4. Trim the units from step 3 to 2½" wide using your ruler and rotary cutter. Make the first cut about ¾" beyond the center points of the fabric as shown. Then reverse the strip and cut the strip 2½" wide.

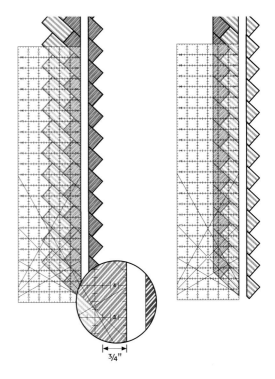

ASSEMBLING THE QUILT TOP

1. Arrange the blocks as shown, or play with the blocks on a design wall to determine a setting that you like. See "Arranging the Blocks" on page 13. Sew the blocks together in eight

horizontal rows of four blocks each. Press the seams in opposite directions from row to row. Join the rows. Press all the seams in one direction.

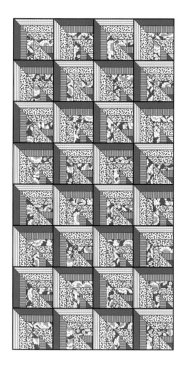

2. Refer to "Adding Borders" on page 14. Measure the length of the quilt through the center. Sew three 2"-wide solid dark blue strips together end to end into one long strip and cut the strip into two borders to fit the quilt. Sew the strips to the sides of the quilt and press the seams toward the borders.

3. Measure the width of the quilt through the center. Piece the remaining 2"-wide dark blue strips, cut two strips to fit and sew them to the top and bottom of the quilt. Press.

4. Measure the quilt through the center to find the width and the length. Cut the strip-pieced border pieces to the lengths measured. Sew a 2½" dark blue corner square to each end of the top and bottom border strips.

5. Sew the pieced border strips to the sides of the quilt. Press the seams toward the solid dark blue inner border. Sew the top and bottom pieced border strips to the quilt. Press toward the inner border.

6. Repeat the measuring and sewing procedure to add the 7½"-wide solid dark blue border strips. Press the seams toward the outer border.

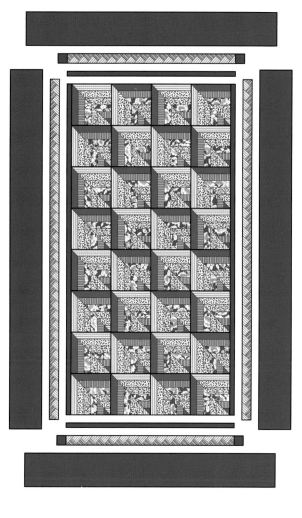

FINISHING THE QUILT

1. Layer the quilt top with batting and backing; baste.

2. Outline quilt the light and dark zigzag lines that oscillate over the quilt. Quilt the first dark blue border ¹⁄₁₆" inside the border. Quilt the outer dark blue border ¹⁄₁₆" inside the border. I used the star quilting pattern on page 75 in the blocks and in the outer border.

3. Attach a hanging sleeve, if desired, referring to "Adding a Hanging Sleeve" on page 18.

4. Use the blue checked strips to bind the edges of the quilt. Refer to "Binding" on page 18.

Breaking Out

By Maaike Bakker and Ineke Jongens, 2004

The narrow orange strips and the blocks that break into the border make this quilt an exciting one. This interesting block design works admirably for a bed quilt as well.

Finished quilt: 41" x 56" ❀ **Finished block:** 7⅛"

MATERIALS

Yardage is based on 42"-wide fabric.

⅝ yard *each* of 6 colors ranging from red to purple to bluish green for blocks

1 yard of bluish green for the border

¼ yard of orange for the accent strips

½ yard of variegated plaid for binding

2⅝ yards of fabric for backing

47" x 62" piece of batting

CUTTING

All measurements include ¼" seam allowances. Before you cut, read "Cutting Strips" on page 8.

From *each* of the 6 colors ranging from red to bluish green, cut:

❋ 9 strips, 1¾" x 42"

From the orange, cut:

❋ 6 strips, 1" x 42"

From the bluish green, cut:

❋ 5 strips, 5½" x 42"

From the variegated plaid, cut:

❋ 3"-wide bias strips to total 206"

MAKING THE BLOCKS

Refer to "Sewing Strip Sets" on page 9 and "Cutting Square Blocks" on page 10.

1. Arrange the six different strips from red to bluish green. Sew the strips together into a strip set as shown. Press the seams toward the darker colors. Make nine strip sets.

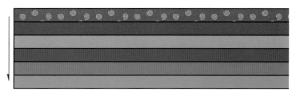

Make 9 strip sets.

2. Trim one of the short sides of each strip set to a 90° angle. Before you cut them into squares, measure the width of the strip sets carefully. If your strip sets are not 8" wide, adjust the measurements to cut squares that are equal to the width of your strip sets. Cut each strip set into 4 squares to yield a total 36 squares (2 of the squares will be extra).

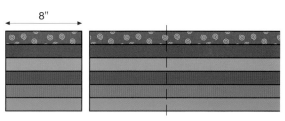

Cut 36 segments.

3. Cut 17 of the squares in half diagonally in one direction; cut another 17 squares in half diagonally in the opposite direction. You'll have 4 different triangles, 17 of each, for a total of 68.

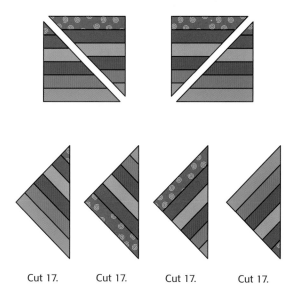

Cut 17.   Cut 17.   Cut 17.   Cut 17.

4. Sew triangles together to make 15 blocks with two red sides and 13 blocks with two bluish green sides. Press the seams open.

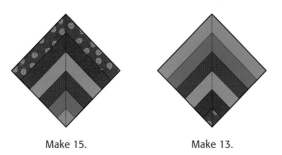

Make 15.   Make 13.

ASSEMBLING THE QUILT TOP

1. Arrange the blocks and triangles as shown, or play with the blocks on a design wall to determine a setting that you like. If you choose the same setting that I chose, sew the blocks together in diagonal rows as shown.

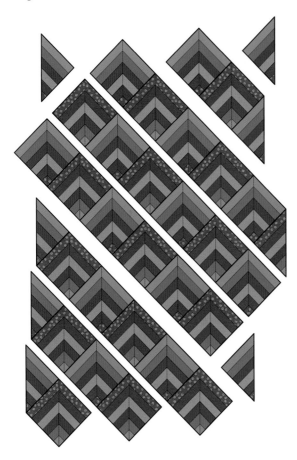

2. Join the three diagonal rows of blocks that create the center "rectangle." Fold and press the orange strips lengthwise, wrong sides together.

Lay one orange strip on each of the four sides of the rectangle and trim the strips to fit. Align the raw edges, and pin. Don't add an orange strip to the short diagonal edge of the rectangle.

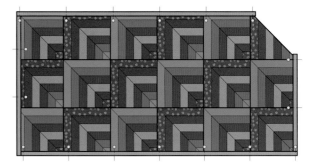

3. Join the rows for the top-right corner section. Trim the extending parts of the blocks along the top edge, leaving ¼" beyond the point of the block for the seam allowance as shown.

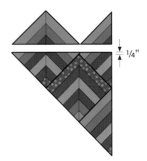

¼"

4. Join the rows for the bottom-left corner section. Add the triangle for the bottom-right corner, but sew a partial seam as shown; don't stitch the entire seam. Trim the extending portions of the blocks along the lower edge, leaving ¼" for the seam allowance.

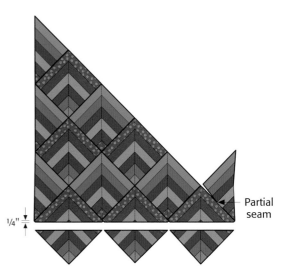

Partial seam

¼"

5. Trim the triangle that will be the upper-left corner, leaving ¼" above the point for the seam allowance.

Trim and discard.

¼"

6. Place the remaining orange strips (folded lengthwise) around the edges of the outer corner sections of the quilt as shown. Trim to fit. Align the raw edges and pin. Sew the 5½"-wide bluish green strips to the corner sections, leaving 6" lengths extending beyond the points. The orange strips will be sewn between the seams. Sew the side strips first, then the top and bottom strips. Press the seam allowances toward the bluish green borders.

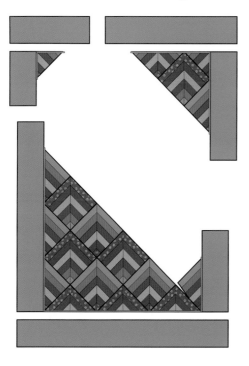

7. Trim the excess border strips at a 45° angle, aligning them with the blocks as shown.

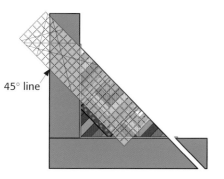

45° line

8. Join the corner sections to the center section in this order: both top corners, the bottom-right corner, and at last the bottom-left corner. You will complete the partial seam when you add the bottom-left corner.

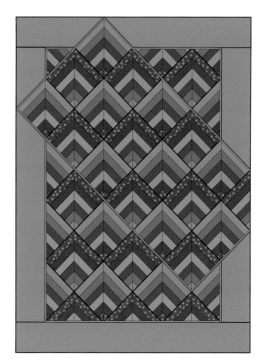

FINISHING THE QUILT

1. Layer the quilt top with batting and backing, baste.

2. Quilt the top lines of the horizontal red and bluish green zigzag lines ¹⁄₁₆" inside the patches. Outline quilt the orange accent strips. Quilt a gold spiral (page 78) in each block by drawing the design on the back side of the quilt, referring to "Quilting 'Upside Down'" on page 17. Wind gold thread on the bobbin and use a yellowish gold thread as the needle thread. The same design is quilted in the bluish green border with bluish green thread.

3. Attach a hanging sleeve, if desired, referring to "Adding a Hanging Sleeve" on page 18.

4. Use the variegated plaid strips to bind the edges of the quilt. Refer to "Binding" on page 18.

Optical Illusion

By Maaike Bakker, Bartina Noorman, and Marijke Schortinghuis, 2004

*This design is very popular among my students, who have made it in many different color combinations.
The range of colors from light to dark and the zigzag placement create the feeling of depth. In this
black-and-white version, there is also the illusion that the vertical rows seem to taper.*

Finished quilt: 68½" x 96" ❋ Finished block: 10" equilateral triangle

MATERIALS

Yardage is based on 42"-wide fabric.

1⅛ yards *each* of 6 fabrics in gradations from white to black for blocks

2 yards of solid black fabric for inner and outer borders

⅜ yard of red fabric for middle border

1 yard of black plaid for binding

6 yards of fabric for backing

75" x 102" piece of batting

CUTTING

All measurements include ¼" seam allowances. Before you cut, read "Cutting Strips" on page 8.

From *each* of the 6 white to black fabrics, cut

❀ 17 strips, 2" x 42"

From the solid black fabric, cut:

❀ 8 strips, 2" x 42"

❀ 8 strips, 6" x 42"

From the red fabric, cut:

❀ 8 strips, 1" x 42"

From the black plaid fabric, cut:

❀ 3"-wide bias strips to total 345"

MAKING THE BLOCKS

Refer to "Sewing Strip Sets" on page 9 and "Cutting 60°-Triangle Blocks" on page 11.

1. Arrange the six different strips from white to black. Sew the strips into a strip set as shown. Press the seams toward the darker colors. Make a total of 17 strip sets.

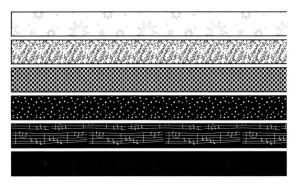

Arrange strips from white to black.

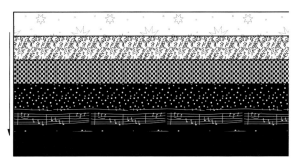

Make 17 strip sets.

2. Place the 60°-angle mark of the ruler on one of the inner seams of the strip set and cut a 60° angle.

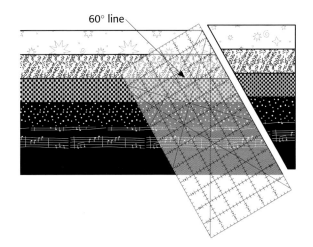

60° line

3. Cut each strip set into six 60° triangles to yield a total of 102 triangles: 51 with a white base and 51 with a black base.

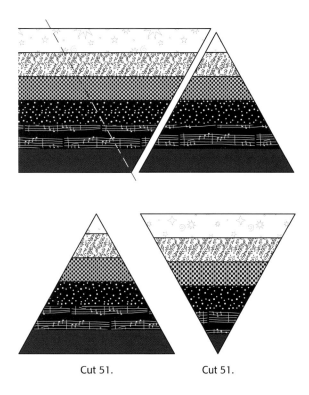

Cut 51.   Cut 51.

ASSEMBLING THE QUILT TOP

1. Arrange the blocks as shown, or play with the blocks on a design wall to determine a setting that you like. See "Arranging the Blocks" on page 13. Make three vertical rows of 17 triangles with a light base and three rows of 17 triangles with a dark base. Sew the blocks into rows. Press toward

the black or white strip. Join the rows and press the seams open.

2. Trim the top and bottom edges of the quilt as shown, allowing ¼" for seam allowances beyond the points.

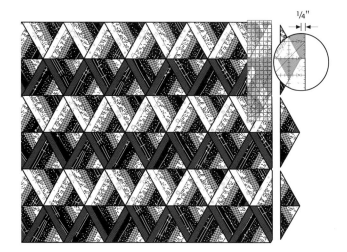

3. Sew the eight 2"-wide solid black strips together in pairs to make four long strips. Refer to "Adding Borders" on page 14. Measure the length of the quilt through the center. Cut two borders to fit the quilt. Sew the strips to the sides of the quilt and press the seams toward the borders.

4. Measure the width of the quilt through the center, including the borders just added . Cut and sew the remaining 2"-wide solid black strips to the top and bottom of the quilt. Press.

5. Repeat the measuring and sewing procedure to add the 1"-wide red strips.

6. Repeat to add the 6"-wide solid black border strips.

FINISHING THE QUILT

1. Layer the quilt top with batting and backing; baste.

2. Outline quilt the light and dark vertical zigzag lines. Quilt a design of circles in the spaces between the zigzag lines. Use a cup and saucer as templates. Mark the circles on the back side of the quilt. Refer to "Quilting 'Upside Down'" on page 17. Outline quilt the red border. Quilt the outer border as shown using a walking foot. Mark the design on the back side of the quilt.

3. Attach a hanging sleeve, if desired, referring to "Adding a Hanging Sleeve" on page 18.

4. Use the black plaid strips to bind the edges of the quilt. Refer to "Binding" on page 18.

Paapje Strips

By Maaike Bakker and Hilly Oosterloo, 2001

Paapje (pronounced POP-yuh) is the name of a Dutch silkscreen studio where beautiful hand-printed fabric is made. The studio is still in operation after more than 80 years, and this quilt is made using the studio's very special fabric.

Finished quilt: 58" x 80½" ❋ Finished block: 7"

MATERIALS

Yardage is based on 42"-wide fabric. Note that the silk-screened fabric used in the quilt shown is not available in the United States. Substitute a bold print or hand-dyed fabric for equally beautiful results.

⅝ yard *each* of 6 colors ranging from pale yellow to green to blue for blocks

1⅞ yards of solid dark blue fabric for inner and outer borders

⅜ yard of green print for middle border

¾ yard of variegated plaid for binding

5 yards of fabric for backing

64" x 87" piece of batting

12 blue buttons, ½" diameter

CUTTING

All measurements include ¼" seam allowances. Before you cut, read "Cutting Strips" on page 8.

From *each* of the 6 colors ranging from pale yellow to blue, cut:

❀ 8 strips, 2¼" x 42"

From the solid dark blue fabric, cut:

❀ 8 strips, 2¼" x 42"

❀ 7 strips, 5½" x 42"

From the green print, cut:

❀ 6 strips, 1¼" x 42"

From the variegated plaid, cut:

❀ 3"-wide bias strips to total 289"

MAKING THE BLOCKS

Refer to "Sewing Strip Sets" on page 9 and "Cutting Square Blocks" on page 10.

1. Arrange the six different yellow to blue strips from light to dark. Sew the strips into a strip set as

shown. Press the seams toward the darker colors. Make eight strip sets.

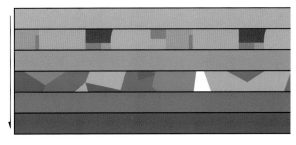

Make 8 strip sets.

2. Trim one of the short sides of each strip set to a 90° angle. Before you cut the squares, measure the width of the strip sets carefully. If your strip sets are not 11" wide, adjust the measurements to cut squares that are equal to the width of your strip sets. Cut each strip set into three squares to yield a total of 24 squares.

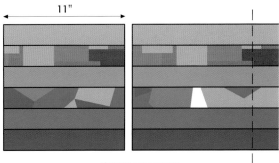

Cut 24 segments.

3. Cut the squares in half twice diagonally. You'll have 4 different triangles, 24 of each for a total of 96. Label the triangles as shown and stack like triangles together.

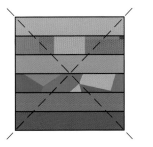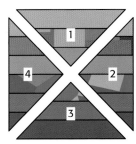

Cut 24 of each.

4. Make 24 blocks using triangles 1 and 2, and 24 blocks using triangles 3 and 4.

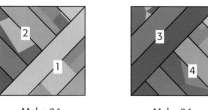

Make 24.   Make 24.

MAKING THE PIECED BORDER

1. Unstitch the center seam of the leftover strip sets from step 2 so that you have three-strip strip sets. Cut these smaller strip sets into 2¼"-wide segments. You need 18 segments of each color combination. Sew the segments together as shown to make a pieced border of lighter segments for the top of the quilt and a pieced border of darker segments for the bottom.

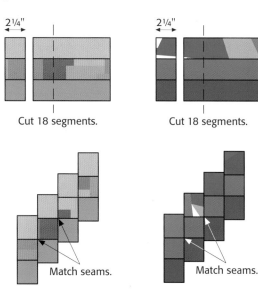

Cut 18 segments.   Cut 18 segments.

Match seams.   Match seams.

2. Trim the pieced borders to be 3" wide, leaving ¼" beyond the points of the center square for the seam allowance.

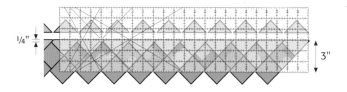

3. Trim a 90° angle on one of the short sides of the border strips and set the border strips aside.

ASSEMBLING THE QUILT TOP

1. Arrange the blocks as shown, or play with the blocks on a design wall to determine a setting that you like. See "Arranging the Blocks" on page 13. Sew the blocks together in horizontal rows. Press the seams open. Join the rows and press.

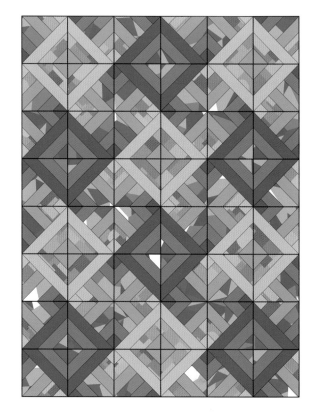

PIN FIRST

When sewing the blocks together, pin them with fine straight pins to help control the bias edges. Sew over the pins carefully, or remove them as you get to them.

2. Refer to "Adding Borders" on page 14. Measure the width of the quilt through the center. Sew the 2¼"-wide dark blue strips together end to end into one long strip and cut two border strips to fit

the quilt. Sew the strips to the top and bottom of the quilt and press the seams toward the borders.

3. Trim the pieced border strips to the same length as the 2¼"-wide dark blue strips. Sew the darker pieced border to the bottom of the quilt and the lighter pieced border to the top. Press the seams toward the dark blue strips.

4. Measure the length of the quilt through the center, including the borders just added. Cut and sew the 2¼"-wide dark blue strips to the sides of the quilt. Press toward the dark blue.

5. Repeat the measuring, cutting, and sewing procedure to add the 2¼"-wide dark blue strips to the top and bottom of the quilt. Press the seams toward the solid borders.

6. Repeat the measuring and sewing procedure to add the 1¼"-wide green strips.

7. Repeat to add the 5½"-wide dark blue strips. Press toward the dark blue border.

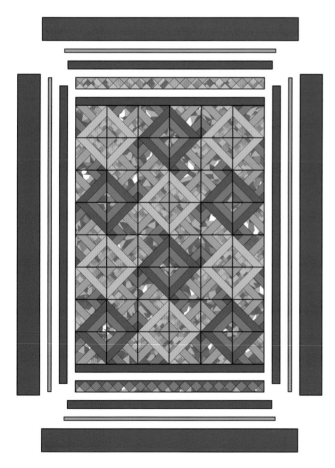

FINISHING THE QUILT

1. Layer the quilt top with batting and backing; baste.

2. Outline quilt the yellow and blue squares both outside and inside the squares. Outline quilt the small green squares between the large yellow and blue squares. Outline quilt the strip-pieced border and the green border. Quilt the large blue border as shown.

3. Sew a blue button in the middle of each yellow and blue square at every other block intersection.

4. Attach a hanging sleeve, if desired, referring to "Adding a Hanging Sleeve" on page 18.

5. Use the variegated plaid strips to bind the edges of the quilt. Refer to "Binding" on page 18.

Falling Leaves

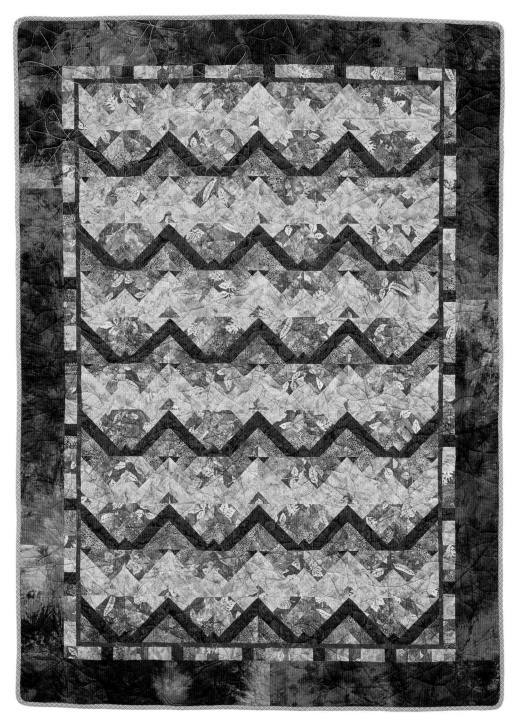

By Maaike Bakker and Frouk van der Molen, 2004

This quilt was inspired by the colors of autumn—rich golds and browns, with a hint of green. The quilt is quilted with an allover design of leaves; the leaves are stitched with threads ranging from yellow in the upper portion of the quilt to brown in the lower part of the quilt.

Finished quilt: 60½" x 83½" ❈ **Finished block:** 5¾"

MATERIALS

Yardage is based on 42"-wide fabric.

1 yard *each* of 6 colors ranging from yellow to dark brown for blocks

1⅜ yards of brown print for outer border

¼ yard of purple fabric for inner border

¾ yard of tan plaid for binding

5 yards of fabric for backing

67" x 90" piece of batting

CUTTING

All measurements include ¼" seam allowances. Before you cut, read "Cutting Strips" on page 8.

From *each* of the 6 colors ranging from yellow to dark brown, cut:

❀ 14 strips, 2" x 42"

From the purple fabric, cut:

❀ 6 strips, 1" x 42"

From the brown print, cut:

❀ 7 strips, 5¾" x 42"

From the tan plaid, cut:

❀ 3"-wide bias strips to total 304"

MAKING THE BLOCKS

Refer to "Sewing Strip Sets" on page 9 and "Cutting Square Blocks" on page 10.

1. Arrange the six different yellow to dark brown strips from light to dark. Sew the strips into a strip set as shown. Press the seams toward the darker colors. Make 14 strip sets.

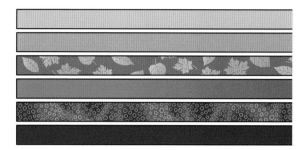

Arrange strips from light to dark.

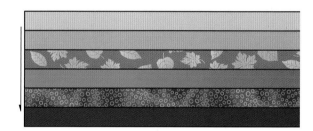

Make 14 strip sets.

2. Trim a short end of each strip set at a 90° angle. Before you cut the squares, measure the width of the strip sets carefully. If your strip sets are not 9½" wide, adjust the measurements to cut squares that are equal to the width of your strip sets. Cut 12 of the strip sets into 4 squares each to yield a total of 48 squares. Set the other 2 strip sets aside for the pieced border.

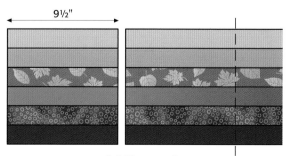

9½"

Cut 48 segments.

3. Cut all the squares in half twice diagonally to yield 192 triangles. Note that each square yields 4 different triangles, for a total of 48 of each. Label the triangles as shown and stack like triangles together.

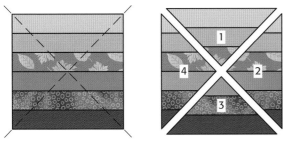

Cut 48 each.

4. Make 24 blocks using triangles 1 and 2, 24 blocks using triangles 1 and 4, 24 blocks using triangles 3 and 4, and 24 blocks using triangles 2 and 3.

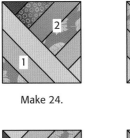

Make 24.   Make 24.

Make 24.   Make 24.

MAKING THE PIECED BORDER

1. Cut the remaining two strip sets into 28 segments, 2" wide.

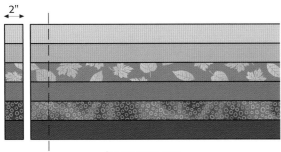

Cut 28 segments.

2. Sew these segments together end to end into four long strips—two that are eight segments long, and two that are six segments long. Set the pieced borders aside.

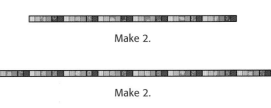

Make 2.

Make 2.

ASSEMBLING THE QUILT TOP

1. Arrange the blocks as shown, or play with the blocks on a design wall to determine a setting that you like. See "Arranging the Blocks" on page 13. Sew the blocks together into 12 horizontal rows of eight blocks each. Press seams open. Join the rows and press.

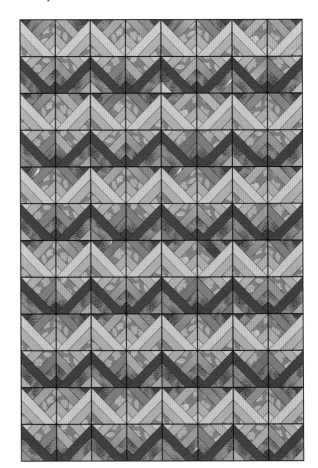

2. Refer to "Adding Borders" on page 14. Measure the length of the quilt through the center. Sew the six 1"-wide purple strips together end to end into a long strip and cut two borders to fit the quilt. Sew the strips to the sides of the quilt and press the seams toward the borders.

3. Measure the width of the quilt through the center, including the borders just added. Cut and sew 1"-wide purple strips to the top and bottom of the quilt. Press.

4. Repeat the measuring, cutting, and sewing procedure to add the strip-pieced borders to the sides of the quilt. Press the seams toward the purple border. Add the pieced border strips to the top and bottom of the quilt and press.

5. Repeat to add the 5¾"-wide brown border strips. Press the seams toward the outer border.

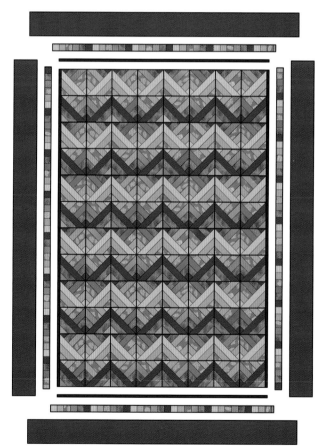

FINISHING THE QUILT

1. Layer the quilt top with batting and backing; baste.

2. Quilt the entire quilt with the free-motion ivy-leaf design on page 79. Enlarge the design using a photocopier; then trace the design onto a sheet of template plastic. Cut out the pattern. Lay the template on the back side of your quilt and trace it with a fabric-marking pencil. Position the leaves randomly all over the quilt. Refer to "Quilting 'Upside Down'" on page 17. Use yellow thread for the leaves in the upper part of the quilt and switch to gradually darker threads as you stitch lower on the quilt, ending with dark brown thread. Quilt the outline of the leaf and the veins. When sewing the veins, you'll sew each line twice.

3. Attach a hanging sleeve, if desired, referring to "Adding a Hanging Sleeve" on page 18.

4. Use the tan plaid strips to bind the edges of the quilt. Refer to "Binding" on page 18.

MAKE YOUR OWN AUTUMN QUILTING DESIGN

Take a leaf, lay it on a piece of paper, and trace around it. Draw a few veins in it. Now you can enlarge the drawing, if needed, with a photocopier. Trace the design onto template plastic and cut out the pattern.

Christmas Stars

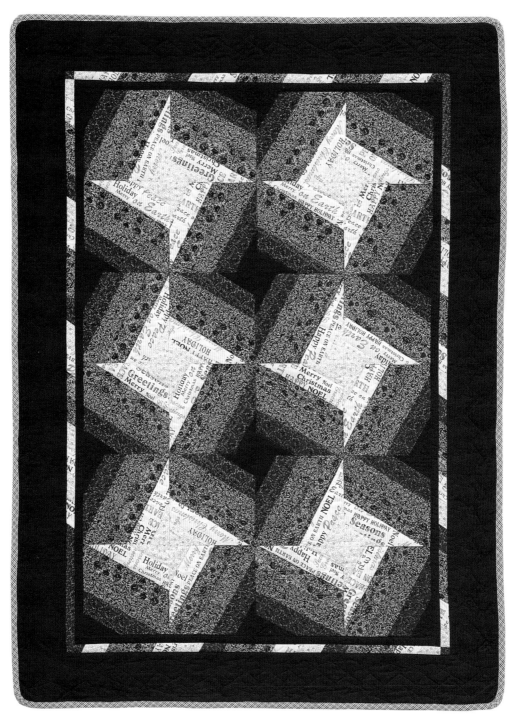

By Maaike Bakker, 2001

This Christmas quilt is simple and fast to make, but it looks complex and sophisticated.
The light prints that you choose will create the light stars, and the darkest
prints will become secondary stars in the background area.

Finished quilt: 42" x 57" ❄ **Finished block: 7½"**

MATERIALS

Yardage is based on 42"-wide fabric.

½ yard *each* of 4 red prints in gradations from medium to dark for blocks

1 yard of dark red solid for inner and outer borders

½ yard *each* of 2 light prints for blocks

⅝ yard of green plaid for binding

2¾ yards of fabric for backing

48" x 63" piece of batting

CUTTING

All measurements include ¼" seam allowances. Before you cut, read "Cutting Strips" on page 8.

From *each* of the 2 light prints and 4 red prints, cut:

❋ 6 strips, 2¼" x 42"

From the dark red solid, cut:

❋ 5 strips, 1¼" x 42"

❋ 5 strips, 4½" x 42"

❋ 4 squares, 1¼" x 1¼"

From the green plaid, cut:

❋ 3"-wide bias strips to total 210"

MAKING THE BLOCKS

Refer to "Sewing Strip Sets" on page 9 and "Cutting Oblique-Square Blocks" on page 12.

1. Arrange the four different red strips from medium to dark. Place two light strips in the top positions as shown. Sew the strips into a strip set as shown.

Press the seams toward the darker colors. Make six strip sets.

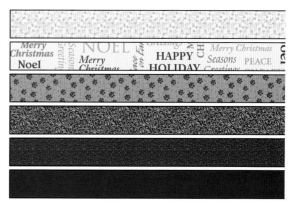

Arrange strips from light to dark red.

Make 6 strip sets.

2. Place a strip set on the cutting mat with the light strips closest to you. Trim the right edge at a 90° angle. Mark a point along the top edge that is 5½" in from the upper-right corner. Cut from this marked point to the lower-right corner.

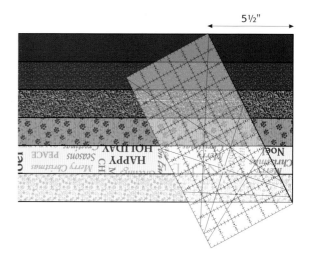

3. Rotate the cutting mat so that the cut end of the strip set is on the left and cut the strip set into four segments that are 8" wide and parallel to the first cutting line. Repeat for each of the strip sets to cut a total of 24 segments.

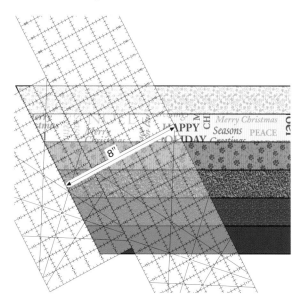

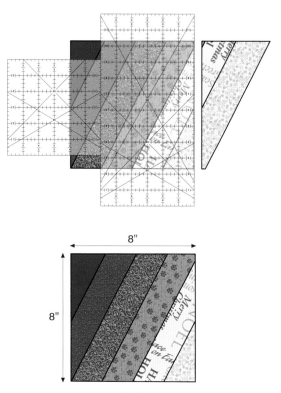

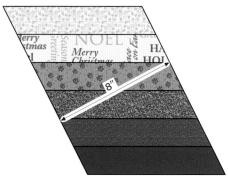

Cut 24.

4. Cut these segments into 8" squares, as shown, to yield 24 blocks.

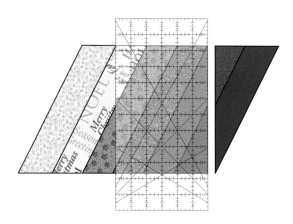

MAKING THE PIECED BORDER

1. Cut the leftovers from the strip sets into 1¼"-wide segments that are parallel to the cutting lines of the blocks. Cut enough segments to total approximately 160".

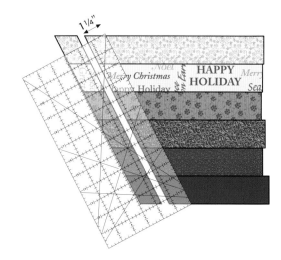

2. Sew the segments together end to end into one long strip.

ASSEMBLING THE QUILT TOP

1. Arrange the blocks as shown, or play with the blocks on a design wall to determine a setting that you like. See "Arranging the Blocks" on page 13. Sew the blocks together in horizontal rows. Press the seams in opposite directions from row to row. Join the rows.

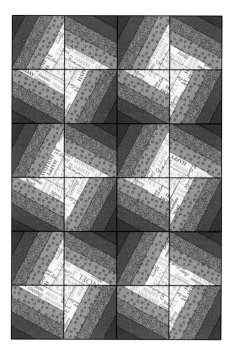

2. Refer to "Adding Borders" on page 14. Measure the length of the quilt through the center. Sew the 1¼"-wide dark red strips together end to end into a long strip and cut two borders to fit the quilt. Sew the strips to the sides of the quilt and press the seams toward the borders.

3. Measure the width of the quilt through the center, including the borders just added. Cut and sew 1¼"-wide dark red strips to the top and bottom of the quilt. Press.

4. Measure the quilt through the center to find the width and the length. Cut the pieced-border strips to the lengths measured. Sew a 1¼" red print square to each end of the top and bottom border strips.

5. Sew the pieced-border strips to the sides of the quilt. Press the seams toward the solid border strips. Sew the pieced-border strips with corner squares to the top and bottom of the quilt and press.

6. Repeat the measuring, cutting, and sewing procedure to add the 4½"-wide dark red border strips. Press the seams toward the outer border.

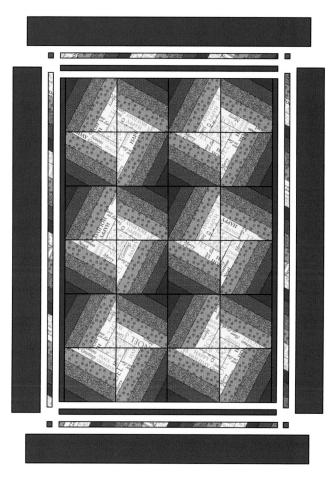

FINISHING THE QUILT

1. Layer the quilt with batting and backing; baste.

2. Outline quilt the inner and outer stars. Fill the dark red areas with stipple quilting. Outline quilt the strip-pieced border. Quilt the outer border with the free-motion star design on page 77.

3. Attach a hanging sleeve, if desired, referring to "Adding a Hanging Sleeve" on page 18.

4. Use the green plaid strips to bind the edges of the quilt. Refer to "Binding" on page 18.

The Amazon

By Maaike Bakker and Els Oosterloo, 2004

We used the same method of strip piecing and cutting for this quilt as we did for
"Christmas Stars" on page 66, but the look is very different. The greens and blues combined
with a diagonal setting transform the quilt into a rainforest crisscrossed by rivers.

Finished quilt: 67¼" x 67¼" ❉ **Finished block:** 7"

MATERIALS

Yardage is based on 42"-wide fabric.

1 yard *each* of 6 colors ranging from light green to bluish green to purple

2 yards of dark purple print for borders

¼ yard of bright pink fabric for borders

¾ yard of variegated plaid for binding

4¼ yards of fabric for backing

74" x 74" piece of batting

CUTTING

All measurements include ¼" seam allowances. Before you cut, read "Cutting Strips" on page 8.

From *each* of the 6 colors ranging from light green to purple, cut:

❈ 14 strips, 2" x 42"

From the dark purple print, cut:

❈ 6 strips, 2" x 42"
❈ 8 strips, 6" x 42"

From the bright pink fabric, cut:

❈ 6 strips, ¾" x 42"

From the variegated plaid, cut:

❈ 3"-wide bias strips to total 282"

MAKING THE BLOCKS

Refer to "Sewing Strip Sets" on page 9 and "Cutting Oblique-Square Blocks" on page 12.

1. Arrange the six different light green to purple strips from light to dark. Sew them into a strip set as shown. Press the seams toward the darker colors. Make 14 strip sets.

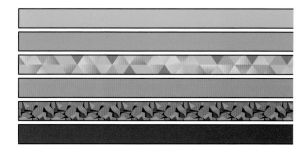

Arrange strips from light green to purple.

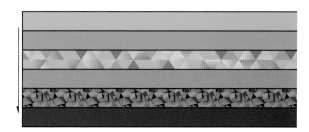

Make 14 strip sets.

2. Place a strip set on the cutting mat with the green strips closest to you. Trim the right edge of the strip to a 90° angle. Mark a point along the top edge that is 2½" from the end. Align the ruler with this mark and the lower-right corner. Cut along the edge of the ruler.

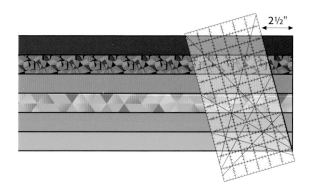

3. Rotate the cutting mat so that the cut end of the strip set is on the left and cut each strip set into 7½" segments that are parallel to the first cutting line. Cut 4 segments each from seven strip sets for a total of 28 segments.

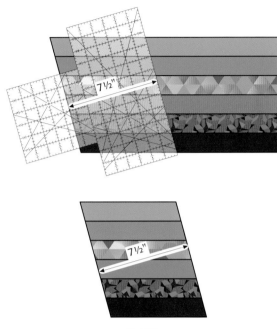

Cut 28.

4. From the remaining seven strip sets, cut 28 segments in reverse. Place a strip set on the cutting mat with the green strips closest to you. Trim the right edge of the strip set to a 90° angle. Mark a point along the bottom edge that is 2½" from the end. Align the ruler with this mark and the upper-right corner. Cut along the edge of the ruler. Rotate the cutting mat so that the cut end of the strip set is on the left and cut each strip set into 7½" segments that are parallel to the first cutting line.

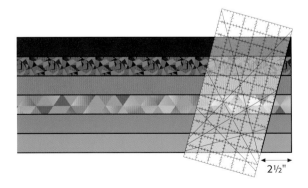

5. Cut the segments from steps 3 and 4 into 56 squares, 7½" x 7½", as shown, 28 and 28 in reverse.

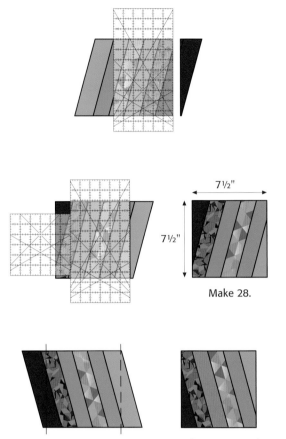

Make 28.

Make 28 reversed.

MAKING THE PIECED BORDER

1. Arrange seven blocks as shown and sew them together.

2. Cut the row lengthwise into four strips, each 1⅞" wide.

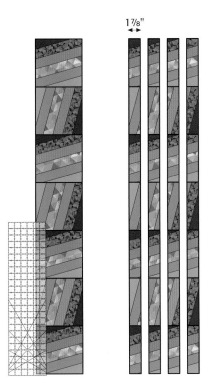

3. Cut four additional 1⅞"-wide segments from the leftovers from the strip sets. Trim the ends to a 90° angle and sew one to each strip from step 2.

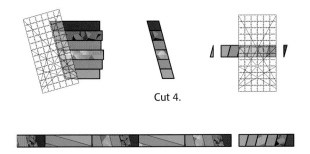

Cut 4.

4. Set the strips aside until you add the borders.

ASSEMBLING THE QUILT TOP

1. Arrange the blocks as shown, or play with the blocks on a design wall to determine a setting that you like. See "Arranging the Blocks" on page 13. Sew the blocks together in horizontal rows. Press the seams in opposite directions from row to row. Join the rows.

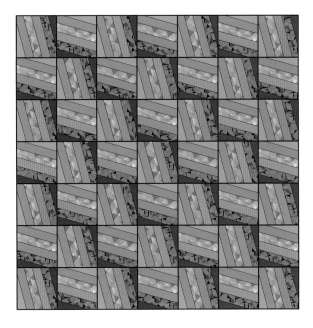

2. Refer to "Adding Borders" on page 14. Measure the length of the quilt through the center. Sew the six 2"-wide purple strips together end to end into a long strip and cut two borders to fit the quilt. Sew the strips to the sides of the quilt and press the seams toward the borders.

3. Measure the width of the quilt through the center, including the borders just added. Cut and sew 2"-wide purple strips to the top and bottom of the quilt. Press.

4. Repeat the measuring and sewing procedure to add the ¾"-wide bright pink strips. Press toward the purple border.

5. Repeat to add the strip-pieced borders to the quilt. Press the seams toward the bright pink borders.

6. Repeat to add the 6"-wide purple strips. Press the seams toward the outer border.

FINISHING THE QUILT

1. Layer the quilt with batting and backing; baste.

2. Quilt the center of the quilt with free-motion diagonal designs, alternating wavy lines with waves as shown. Quilt the center of the quilt $\frac{1}{16}$" inside the seam of the 1½"-wide purple border. Outline quilt the bright pink border. Quilt the 5½" purple border $\frac{1}{16}$" inside the seam of the strip-pieced border, and quilt the same waves as in the center.

3. Attach a hanging sleeve, if desired, referring to "Adding a Hanging Sleeve" on page 18.

4. Use the variegated plaid strips to bind the edges of the quilt. Refer to "Binding" on page 18.

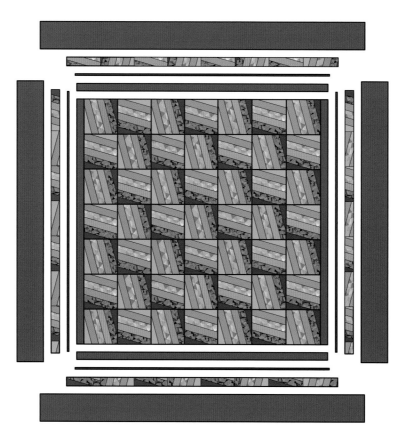

Quilting Designs

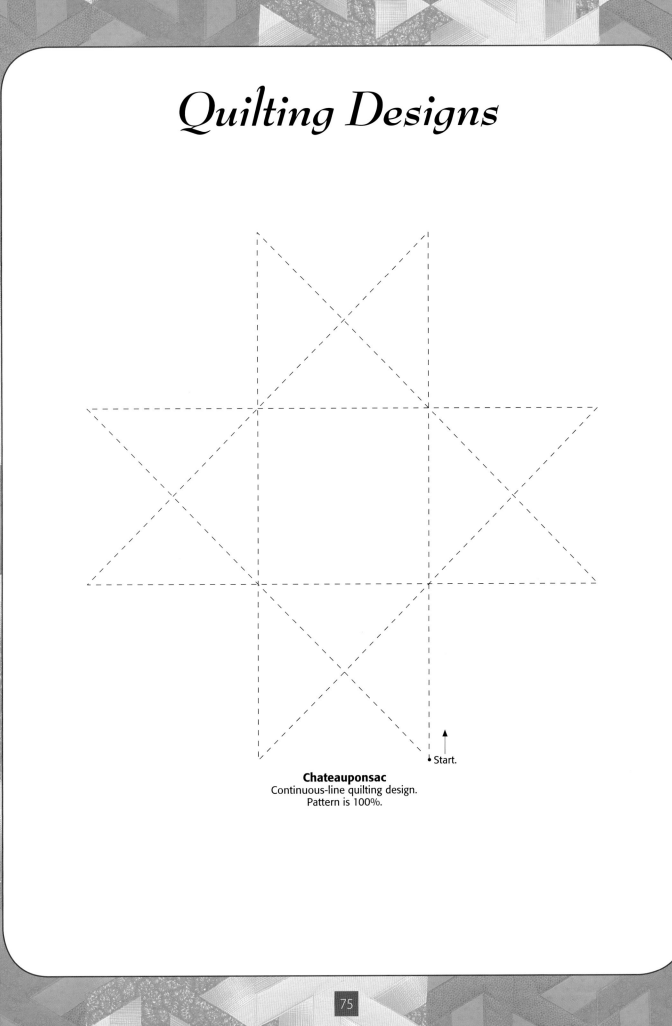

Start.

Chateauponsac
Continuous-line quilting design.
Pattern is 100%.

Crib Quilt 1
Continuous-line quilting designs.
Enlarge patterns 150%.

Crib Quilt 2
Continuous-line quilting design.
Enlarge pattern 150%.

Good Night
Continuous-line quilting design.
Pattern is 100%.

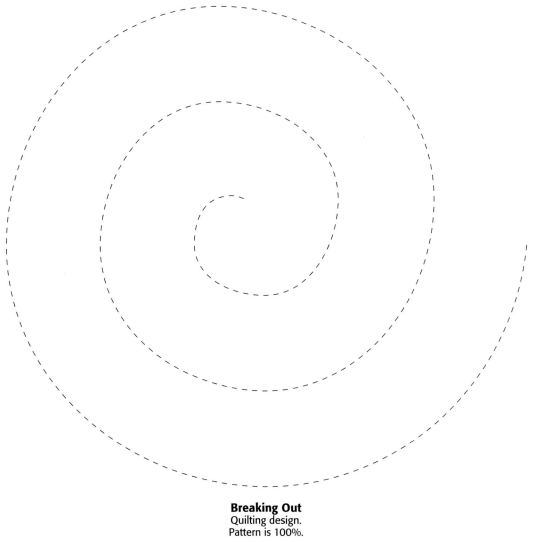

Breaking Out
Quilting design.
Pattern is 100%.

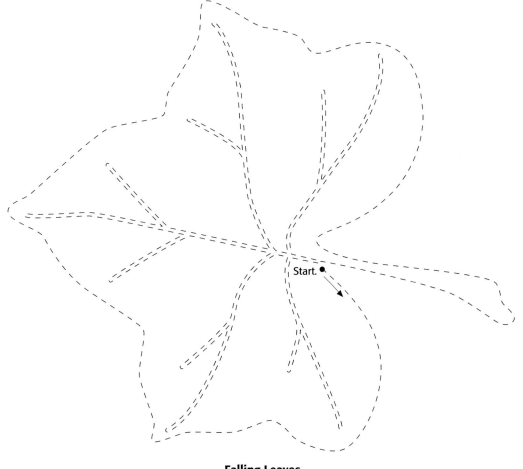

Start.

Falling Leaves
Quilting design.
Enlarge pattern 200%.

About the Author

Maaike Bakker was born in 1958 in the Netherlands. She studied textile techniques and art history at a teacher-training college and at an art academy. In 1978 she created her first quilt as a wedding gift for close friends. After a visit to Virginia and North Carolina in 1993, she became very enthusiastic about paper piecing and foundation piecing. In 1997 she published her first book, *Paper Piecing,* in the Netherlands. This is her second book with Martingale & Company.

Maaike lives and works in a little village in the north of the Netherlands. In her studio in an old farmhouse, she designs her quilts and writes books and articles. She also teaches patchwork techniques in her studio to many groups and individuals. She has been invited several times to teach classes in Germany and France.

Many of her quilts have been exhibited in the Netherlands, Germany, and the United States.

Maaike and her husband, Theo, who does the word processing and the first editing of her books, have three children: two daughters (ages 23 and 14) and one son (age 20). Both daughters like patchwork and quilting too.

For more information, visit Maaike's Web site: www.ateliermaaikebakker.nl.